With thanks
for your friendship
and most gracious
hospitality
Donny and Carey
Head
07/29/2012

D1133097

NO TURNING BACK

The Art of Veryl Goodnight

Veryl Goodnight

Published by Goodnight Fine Art, Ltd.

www.verylgoodnight.com

(970) 533-1172

Printed in the United States of America
Cover photograph by Mike White
Design by Laura McCurdy
Printing by O'Neil Printing, Phoenix, AZ
Binding by Roswell Bookbinding, Phoenix, AZ

NO TURNING BACK

The Art of Veryl Goodnight

This book is dedicated to
my husband, Roger Brooks,
for his rock solid judgment and
his compassion for humanity

and

To the animals
with whom we share this earth

Contents

Preface

This book coincides with a forty-year retrospective of my work at the Thomas Gilcrease Museum in Tulsa, Oklahoma, April 2011. In addition to being an art book, it is a thank you to the hundreds of people that have stepped up over the years to support my work. This book recognizes many of the people and animals that have inspired me to create.

I am not able to mention each one of you by name, but perhaps you will remember reaching out to me somewhere along the journey and you may recognize your own fingerprint on a particular sculpture or painting. If you ever shared a story, a photograph, a prop, an animal, or modeled for me, you were part of my creative process.

If you are among the many artists who have been generous with your own knowledge, you have been a vital inspiration. If you bought my work or helped secure a public placement, you enabled me to create my next sculpture. If you sold my work, wrote an article or even spoke a few words mentioning my art, you encouraged the next piece. If you worked in a foundry, a gallery, volunteered at an art show, or simply complimented my work, you are part of this story.

The saying, "It takes a village to raise a child," is equally applicable to an artist's career. This book is my thanks to you, my Village.

Veryl

Foreword

Modeled On Life, The Art of Veryl Goodnight

by James Nottage

As these words are being written, artist Veryl Goodnight works in the barn-studio at her Mancos, Colorado home. She is excited, as always, about her work, and inspiration feeds the idea that will result in a new piece for her up-coming show at the Gilcrease Museum in Tulsa, Oklahoma. Having recently visited a museum on the Utah and Wyoming border, she has contemplated words she found there in a pioneer woman's diary. Those words, "Hidden Strength" will be the title of the piece. Later, visiting an antique shop with her good friend, Wayne Wolfe, Veryl leaves with an ancient scythe that, posed with model Hillary Ross, will help to convey the wind-blown look of the figure in the sculpture. It will be a quiet homage to the women who settled the West. For the 40 year retrospective exhibit at the Gilcrease and to fully appreciate Veryl Goodnight, "Hidden Strength" is also an apt description of the artist herself.

The book you hold in your hands is the honest and open story of Veryl Goodnight's journey as a person and as an artist. One should contemplate, however, not just how her work has grown and developed over the years. The personal story since the early 1970s runs in concert with pivotal years in the story of the field of Western art itself. In the early 1970s, many of the artists we consider to be "masters" in the field were still active and producing some of their best work. Olaf Wieghorst, John Clymer, Tom Lovell, Robert Lougheed, Bettina Steinke, Gerard Curtis Delano, and many others were showing at galleries and exhibits as the field flourished. Some were senior members of the field, some were younger, all are now gone. The youngsters coming along learned directly from them and benefited from the enthusiasm of their patrons and their success. The Cowboy Artists of America organization was only a few years old and had its first show at the newly dedicated Cowboy Hall of Fame in 1966. The major commercial shows and sales were in prominent galleries such as Trailside in Scottsdale and Jackson Hole.

Think more about what had not happened by the early 1970s. The National Museum of Wildlife Art, the Autry Museum, the Eiteljorg, the Booth, The Petrie Institute of Western American Art, The Charles M. Russell Center For the Study of Art of the West, the Stark Museum of Art and other important institutions did not exist yet and for the most part had not even been considered by their founders. The Masters of the American West, Quest for the West, and the Buffalo Bill Art Show and

Sale are among those museum sales shows that had not yet been invented. The social centers of Western art activity were Jackson Hole, Scottsdale, Oklahoma City, and Great Falls. Scholarship in the field was primarily being produced with accompanying exhibitions and catalogs by the Amon Carter Museum in Fort Worth and the Buffalo Bill Historical Center in Cody. Specialty commercial houses selling historical and contemporary realist art were not on the scene, but in time the Scottsdale, Jackson Hole, Santa Fe, and Coeur d'Alene art auctions would be leading the field, wresting business from established houses in the East.

In the early 1970s, there was a comparatively small shelf of books devoted to art and artists of the West. Since then, there has been a growing library of publications supporting the field. In fact, the literature has expanded without restraint to include casual picture books, biographies, promotional sales material, and at last a rich library of interpretive studies that explore the art from many angles. When asked why it was time for a book about her career, Veryl Goodnight responds that on the occasion of the Gilcrease show she feels it is a good time to thank the large cast of individuals who have helped her along the way, to pull the elements of her career together into one place. As hundreds of these friends and colleagues know, Veryl is intensely loyal to the collectors, galleries, fellow artists and others who have influenced her along the way. As is expressive of the focus in all her work she offers this book "to help others understand how much she loves animals and history." It is compiled to provide understanding of the artist, her motivations, her struggles, and her triumphs. More importantly, on that combined bookshelf of books in the field, it is a place where you can see the artist in the context of the art world in which she has played a very important part.

Veryl Goodnight was not alone when she began her career painting in a small studio in Denver, struggling to succeed at depicting wildlife and horses. At the same time there was a coterie of artists, older and more established, also struggling in their own way. In the pages that follow, you will read about how Goodnight was influenced by the teaching, coaching and support of James Disney, Ned Jacob, Ken Bunn, George Carlson, Kent Ullberg, Fritz White, Jon Zahourek and many others. She describes herself as being "humble and hungry." It meant the world to her when she was invited to participate in the Northwest Rendezvous, and to work with Gary Carter and other artists in the field sketching live models. Becoming a part of the Trailside Gallery roster of artists, first under Ginger Renner, and then with Ted and Christine Mollring marked a major point of growth. Imagine the quiet sense of overwhelming satisfaction she must have felt, being exhibited in a show alongside Robert Bateman and Harry Jackson!

In a recent interview, Veryl Goodnight confessed that this early accomplishment fulfilled her definition of success at the time, being with an important gallery and showing with such important artists. With a humble expression of thanks, she notes, however, that it was sculptor Kent Ullberg who set her to thinking even more seriously about her work. At that time, a goal she had was to be the best woman sculptor possible. She now focused on being the best artist she could be without reference to gender. It was a pivotal moment when she grew to recognize that the key to successful work was the importance of understanding anatomy. She describes how "the work of both George Carlson and Ken Bunn had loose impressionistic surfaces over solid anatomical foundations. I realized that sculpting every hair was not necessary or even desired." Similar lessons were learned by studying the work of A. Phimister Proctor and his masterful sculptures in Denver, across from the state capital. Lounging at the Jackson Lake Lodge she did detailed sketches from the inspiring wildlife paintings of Carl Rungius. She visited Brookgreen Gardens in South Carolina to study American sculpture and constantly focused upon sculptural depictions of the horse. At some expense she attended every exhibit of the Cowboy Artists of America and the National Academy of Fine Art. She learned from the best of role models, holding the likes of Tom Lovell and John Clymer in very high regard.

One thing that never caused Veryl Goodnight to hesitate was the idea of being a woman in a male-dominated genre of art. She simply knew that in order succeed, she had to meet or exceed the standards of any other artist. She recognized that her work, to be taken seriously, also had to avoid being cute or sweet. Even when sculpting young animals, she had to approach her subject "from a naturalist's point of view." A youthful ambition imagined her being a member of the Cowboy Artists of America, even though they did not allow women members.

One of the most profound works in Veryl Goodnight's oeuvre is *The Day the Wall Came Down,* one of the great allegorical equestrian sculptures, the very definition of freedom. At the same time, this is not a singular work for the artist in that much of her art has messages going well beyond the depiction of wildlife or pioneer women. It is the later subject that began as a series for her in about 1984. The first was *Cares for Her Brothers*, a sculpture of a woman cradling a young fawn. This view of women as a part of history and as being close to the earth and close to animals is one that has been beautifully portrayed in nearly thirty sculptures so far. From them all, one gains a sense of determination, devotion, and of self and mutual reliance between humans and nature. When the artist began the transition from focusing upon painting to sculpting, she found the ideal medium for conveying motion and emotion with story lines that are enduring. Commenting for an *Art of the West* writer, she stated that "When I'm focused on sculpture, I'm focused on 360 degrees and movement. Sculpture is very factual, painting is very illusionary.

I have a much greater ability to make a statement through movement and body language with my sculpture than with painting."

You can understand this statement in your first view of this book. The title and image of *No Turning Back* are from one of Veryl Goodnight's most memorable works. It is the ideal image of a young woman going west, full of fear and doubt, but determined and gaining self-assurance. Yes, it says something about pioneer ideals, but while it was not intended as a self-portrait, it does in many ways symbolize its creator. It is her sense about art as needing to have a level of adventure, history, and wisdom. That is Veryl Goodnight. She writes in this volume that

"I suppose I envision myself as a pioneer woman, living close to the land and sharing my life with animals. The animal/human relationship has always been important to me." More than that, as an artist she learned long ago the importance of working with live models. Her depictions represent life, taken from life, both human and animal, with sympathy and understanding. As Goodnight commented to author Gretchen Reynolds, writing for *Southwest Art*, "my particular interest is in animals, man, and animals with man. . . . [animals] have intelligence, emotions, and souls. They are our companions on this earth."

As we view the life and work of Veryl Goodnight over the last four decades, we recognize that she has been an essential part of American representational art. In the Western genre, she has been present as a participant in virtually all those shows that did not exist when she started. She is a valued and recognized participant and is represented at most of the museums, shows, and auctions that did not exist in the early 1970s. At that time, she and Glenna Goodacre were among the only women sculptors in the field. Since then, the field has grown so that women are well-represented in almost all venues, mostly on an equal footing with men.

The long-term impact of any artist can be measured in a number of ways. The first is to consider the presence of the artist's work in museum and other public collections. The list of monumental works at the end of this volume is testimony to Veryl Goodnight's success. Another measure is the range of private collectors of note, and many of them are publicly thanked in this book. A third measure is whether or not an artist has had an impact as an example and as a teacher of others, and Veryl Goodnight has taught and encouraged many students over the years. Finally, at the point of this book's publication is the unknown measure of what Goodnight will still accomplish. She has always been prolific. Her imagination seems to be without bound. She is constantly inspired by the landscape, the people, and the creatures that are part of her world. She has modeled all of her work on life in one form or another, and it is the artist's profound respect for life that makes her a model for us all.

James Nottage serves at the Eiteljorg Museum of American Indians and Western Art as Vice President and Chief Curatorial Officer and Gund Curator of Western Art. He earned undergraduate and graduate degrees at the University of Wyoming and a graduate degree in museum studies in New York at the Cooperstown Graduate Program. He first met Goodnight when serving as founding chief curator at what was then the Autry Museum of Western Heritage and has closely followed her work since. He has edited, written, or contributed to more than a dozen books in the fields of Western and American Indian history and art.

Introduction

by Christine Mollring

My husband, Ted, and I will never forget meeting Veryl Goodnight at our first National Academy of Western Art show at the National Cowboy Hall of Fame in Oklahoma City around 1972. We had just arrived at the Lincoln Plaza Hotel when Ted looked out the window and spotted a beautiful girl wearing an orange bathing suit (although over the years and with some embellishment, Ted has been calling it an orange bikini!). Ted then informed me that he did not feel like unpacking, and that he was going to the pool to read the newspaper. He had not been there but for a few minutes when the beautiful girl in the orange bathing suit approached Ted and said, "Are you Mr. Mollring? My name is Veryl Goodnight. I am an artist and I understand that you and your wife, Christine, just purchased Trailside Galleries." Indeed, Ted and I had just purchased the gallery in 1971, and while Veryl had been represented by Trailside Galleries prior to our ownership, upon seeing her work Ted and I soon asked her to join our stable of artists. Thus began an enduring artist-dealer relationship and friendship. We then asked Veryl to be included in a three-person exhibition with two well-known artists we represented at that time—the Canadian Wildlife artist Robert Bateman and the renowned sculptor from Cody, Wyoming, Harry Jackson. The show was a major success, and Veryl's career was launched.

Prior to our purchase of Trailside Galleries, I managed the Rendezvous Galleries on the north side of the Jackson Town Square in Jackson, Wyoming, during the 1960s and 1970s. When I joined the gallery, Rendezvous only represented and displayed the work of one artist, Carl Roters, from Syracuse, New York. Despite my diverse business experience, this was my first exposure to the fine art and gallery profession, and it was here that I became deeply interested in art and the managements of artists's careers. I then became the Director of the Jensen Galleries in Jackson, which was just down the boardwalk from Trailside Galleries. When I heard that Trailside Galleries was for sale, Ted and I immediately jumped at the exciting opportunity, took a deep breath, and as the saying goes, the rest is history.

The relationship between artists and galleries was quite different in those days. As a gallery, we were prepared to promote an artist's career with advertising and brochures, and when possible, we would include them in two-man or three-man exhibitions. We also worked to expand the scope and market of our gallery audience for our artists by opening other Trailside Galleries locations in the Scottsdale Civic Center Mall in Arizona; the lobby of the Four Seasons Hotel in Houston, Texas; and in Terminal 3 of the Phoenix Sky Harbor International Airport in Arizona. We worked diligently to stay in constant communication with our artists and to help them whenever necessary. In essence, Ted and I viewed the gallery and our artists as one large, extended family. We not only worked with these artists to promote their work and further their careers, but we also cared for them and their families. We counted the artists, as we still do today, among our dear friends, including Veryl and her husband, Roger.

Ted and I viewed the opening receptions for the artists's exhibitions as not only exciting opportunities to view the newest works by the artists, but also as a reunion of sorts with our gallery family. After a group exhibition in either our Scottsdale or Jackson galleries, we held a reception and dinner in our home for the artists and their best collectors. These dinners were inevitably fun and joyous occasions. During the summers in Jackson, we also organized horseback rides and float trips down the Snake River, pancake breakfasts the morning after the exhibitions, as well as picnics and other activities for the artists and their families. We are proud that these events have become a Trailside Galleries tradition that continues to this day.

We had a lot of laughs over the years and I recall a very funny episode with Veryl when I hosted a luncheon for her at the Jackson Hole Golf and Tennis Club. I invited the wives of some of Veryl's foremost collectors and I had ordered a very special berry dessert that sounded delicious. However, at some point after we ate dessert, we all went into hysterics when we discovered that we all had purple tongues from the berries! Veryl has always been very lively and we have never forgotten this humorous incident.

Fortunately, Veryl has been loyal to Trailside Galleries since our initial meeting, and she has been represented by the gallery longer than any other artist. In September 2001, Trailside Galleries held a one-woman exhibition for Veryl that was a triumph. Veryl's work speaks to her passion for animals, history, and family, as well as to her tenacious spirit. She must be commended for her perseverance in furthering her career in what was then a male-dominated field. At one time, it was difficult to sell work by a female artist at the gallery, and I recall that Veryl and Glenna Goodacre were the only two women receiving recognition for their sculpture for quite some time. This has changed, of course, and Veryl's drive and determination helped lead the way for other talented women artists who have followed in her footsteps.

Veryl's choice of subject matter has always been driven by her passion for animals and family. Since childhood, Veryl has particularly loved horses, and some of her seminal pieces are equine depictions. Veryl's piece, *The Day the Wall Came Down*, is the manifestation of a dream she had of horses leaping over a representation of the Berlin Wall. Her choice to portray a group of galloping horses symbolized human triumph over politically imposed constraints upon liberty. *The Day the Wall Came Down* is a monumental piece, weighing nearly seven tons, and it is now permanently installed at the George Bush Presidential Library at Texas A&M University in College Station, Texas. A sister casting of the piece was unveiled in front of the Allied Museum in Berlin, Germany, in 1998.

Another major element in Veryl's work is family, and more specifically, her own ancestry. Her exploration into the roots of her surname led Veryl on a journey that profoundly affected her and her work. Charles Goodnight, the famous Texas cattle baron, is her distant relative. After reading about Charles

Ginger Renner, Veryl Goodnight, Christine Mollring and Maryvonne Leshe at Trailside Galleries, Jackson, September 2001.

and his crusade to save the buffalo, Veryl discovered that it was actually Charles's wife, Mary Ann Goodnight, who persuaded her husband to rescue the buffalo calves from the predatory hunters near their ranch. Veryl found a heroine and kindred spirit in Mary Ann, or "Molly" as her husband called her, to whom she was also related, and thus was born *Back from the Brink*. Mary Ann Goodnight is the inspiration for and subject of this piece, which marked a real turning point in Veryl's life and career. Because Veryl works from life rather than photography in order to achieve a heightened realism and accuracy of detail, she chooses live models in the studio. This is when Veryl met Charlie, a buffalo calf that served as the model for this piece.

Veryl had been looking for a buffalo calf as a model for *Back from the Brink*. A friend and orthopedic surgeon, Dr. Marlo Gobel, called one day to inform Veryl about Charlie, who had been orphaned. Veryl and her husband, Roger, flew Charlie home in Roger's plane, falling in love with him along the way. Charlie soon became a part of their family. In fact, when Ted and I once visited Veryl and Roger at their then-home just outside of Santa Fe, New Mexico, we could not believe it when we saw Charlie inside Veryl's studio lying on the couch! Raising Charlie certainly marked a turning point in Veryl's and Roger's lives, as having him led them to move to Colorado and contributed to Veryl's return to wildlife subject matter in her sculpture and painting.

In her explorations of Western subjects, Veryl has found self-expression and compassion and has discovered unique parallels between herself and the women who first settled in the West. Certainly, Veryl sensed a strong connection to Mary Ann Goodnight, but she also realized how important the connection between humans and animals was at that time. Women, in particular, forged strong relationships with their farm animals, finding them to be companions on their quiet, desolate homesteads. These women were of strong character, for they were pioneering new land, new homes, and new lives in the West, where life required self-reliance and gritty resilience. Veryl began to explore portrayals of these pioneer women, often depicting them with animals, leading to her *Women of the West* series. These animals sustained pioneer women not only physically, but also emotionally, and Veryl soon found that animals had that role in her own life. It is clear that Veryl not only feels a connection to these indomitable women for their love of animals, but also for their adventurous and dogged spirits. These women left the comforts of society for the romance of the West, and the series suggests Veryl's own career—her fortitude and perseverance to create the work she wanted to make, to live with and among her animals, and to be one of the most successful female Western sculptors working today. In fact, the title of this book, *No Turning Back*, is an apt description of Veryl's career.

Ted and I are so very happy that Veryl is receiving the distinguished honor and recognition she deserves with her retrospective exhibition at the Gilcrease Museum in Tulsa, Oklahoma. Running concurrently will be an exhibition of another recognized and loyal artist of Trailside Galleries, Curt Walters, who is also a good friend. Veryl and Curt are most deserving of these exhibitions, and for their tireless efforts to capture the spirit, beauty, and grandeur of the American West.

There is a fragment of Veryl in each of the subjects she has elected to explore. Her choice to portray the horses she so adores—those symbols of such strength and grace—is perhaps rooted in Veryl's very nature. Her pioneer women are determined, yet nurturing, and they are nearly metaphorical images of herself, while Veryl's wildlife sculptures are reflective of her deeply personal relationship to all living creatures. Veryl applies a steadfast determination to her work through her attention to anatomical and historical accuracy and to her choice of subject matter. She finds a freedom in her sculpture because she remains true to the tenets of her own work philosophy: to create that which she loves. It is this devotion to her work that allows it to resonate so deeply. Yet Veryl constantly pushes herself technically and artistically, and for the last decade she has delved back into painting, a medium she explored early in her career before she worked in sculpture. Working in the two media is vastly different, but Veryl continuously challenges herself as an artist, which is a testament to her extraordinary talent. She is a wonderfully creative and productive artist who is so richly deserving of her remarkable career, and while we have been granted glimpses of Veryl through her work, this marvelous monograph reveals the heart and soul of an artist whose work has enriched and captivated the lives of so many.

Christine Mollring is a private art consultant who divides her time between Wyoming and Arizona with her husband, Ted. She and her husband owned and operated Trailside Galleries in Jackson, Wyoming, and Scottsdale, Arizona, from 1971 until 1994. Christine has been a judge for the National Cowboy and Western Heritage Museum, Oklahoma City; the Charles M. Russell Museum, Great Falls, Montana; and Arts in the Parks, Jackson, Wyoming. In addition, she has been a guest curator, served on the Board of Trustees, and is the past Chairman of the Art Acquisition Committee at the Desert Caballeros Western Museum in Wickenburg, Arizona.

Presently Christine is actively involved on the Board of Trustees of the Scottsdale Museum of the West in Scottsdale, Arizona and is also Emeritus Member of the Board of the University of Wyoming Art Museum, Laramie, Wyoming. She is also a member of the National Advisory Board of National Museum of Wildlife Art, Jackson Hole, Wyoming.

The dream is in the mind.

Realization is in the hands.

Louis L'Amour

Inspired photo by Claude Steelman

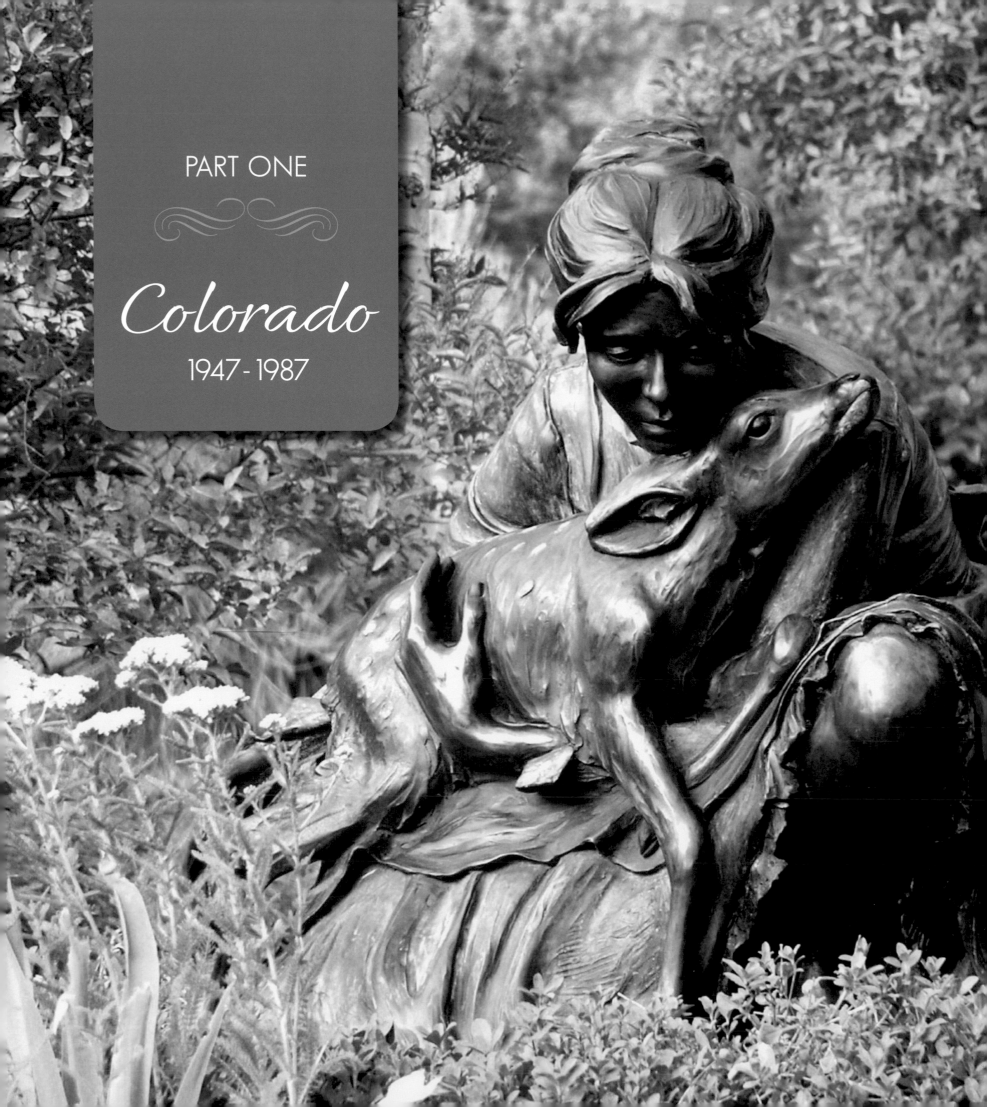

PART ONE

Colorado

1947 - 1987

Childhood

Veryl, Rose, and Bruce Goodnight

I must have been born loving horses. I was told my first spoken word was "Italian," as I excitedly pointed to a horse. It is this love for horses and all other animals, plus a childhood in the Colorado mountains that inspires my art.

My father Dale Goodnight worked for Continental Oil Company. Until I started first grade, my childhood home was the cab of a Chevy pick up truck and hotels in small Colorado towns. Dad, my mother Rose and my baby brother, Bruce traveled from small town to small town across the state so Dad could build gasoline storage "bulk plants" and new filling stations for Conoco. When I began first grade in 1956, we settled into a trailer near my grade school in Lakewood, Colorado. Dad would leave early on Monday and be back home by Friday afternoon, bearing gifts for Bruce and me. Weekends were spent helping to construct our new home on 18th and Ingalls Street, strategically located between the grade school, the junior high school and Jefferson County High School.

My parents loved to go fishing and hunting in the Colorado mountains. I resisted the hunting from a very early age and even rescued freshly caught fish to be released back into the rivers. I was finally excused from the hunting trips; however, they left me with a love and longing for aspens and mountain meadows. It wasn't until October 2006 that the dream to actually live in the Colorado mountains was realized.

Mom would save pennies from her grocery budget to insure that I had art supplies and a collection of Foster's *How To Draw* books. I still remember my first oil painting set under the Christmas tree. I immediately began painting the horse I couldn't otherwise have. Every winter our front yard was filled with sculpted snow horses. I would ride them and cry when they melted. I often wonder if my artistic talent would have developed if I could have had a real horse.

We were still living at Mitchell Trailer Court when we got our first television set. My folks managed to get one for us in 1953 when I was six years old. Programs such as *Lassie*, *Rin Tin Tin*, *My Friend Flicka* and *Fury* all fueled my passion for dogs and horses.

Dale Goodnight

Detail from *Shepherds of the High Plains*. Veryl's father Dale Goodnight modeled as the shepherd.

I believe that the Western classics had a profound effect on the entire Baby Boomer Generation. I am not the only one who has always longed to live on a "ranch" and have horses.

When I was a senior in high school, a real western hero was on the television screen. Barbara Stanwyk played the role of Victoria Barkley on *The Big Valley*. She was beautiful and strong, the undisputed matriarch of the ranch and family. I cannot help but wonder how much of her character has influenced my view of women of the West, for I always choose to portray a strong but feminine woman.

We simply did not have the means to support a horse, but I desperately wanted a dog. When in sixth grade, I entered a fire prevention poster contest. My Dad promised me a puppy if I won – against my Mother's wishes. The teacher announced my second place winning during the last class of the day. I was crying so hard, she let me go home early. I ran the entire eight blocks and burst through the door, still crying, to announce that I could get a puppy. Dad kept his promise, and my little dachshund, Gretchen, became the subject of many paintings.

Gretchen's registered name was "Gretchen Gutenacht." My Dad explained that we had a famous ancestor whose picture was hanging in the Cowboy Hall of Fame, Colonel Charles Goodnight. "Gutenacht" is the German word for Goodnight. I loved the idea that I was the descendent of a real cowboy!

*It is absolutely impossible for me to separate my art
from my love for animals,
the Rocky Mountains,
and the unique American history of the West.*

Veryl holding her baby brother Bruce

Detail of *Paint Mare and Filly*, 1987

*Shepherds of the
High Plains,* 1986,
23 x 34 x 20 inches

Social and Artistic Influences
The 1960'S and 1970's

From first grade through high school, I was known as the "class artist". My first art shows were on the front of the family refrigerator. I was involved with every school project that called for art. I showed my paintings at shopping center sidewalk shows, often winning awards.

It was "conventional wisdom" during the 1950's and 1960's that you couldn't make a living as an artist, particularly if you were a woman. If you were brash enough to entertain the thought of an art career, it would definitely require foregoing a husband and family. My parents were very supportive, and I had an equally supportive boyfriend in Larry Weant, so conventional wisdom did not make sense to me. After all, I had been selling my art since I was four years old. Granted, my parents were the collectors, but that sense of success given to a young child can make a deep impression. It instills the confidence needed to succeed.

I was a top student and had a potential art scholarship to the University of Colorado in Boulder. While roadblocks for women were coming down, the abstract art movement was in full force. This was an art form that held no interest for me. My Dad's wisdom was for me to attend business school, so "I always had something to fall back on," and to take evening classes with artists whose work I admired.

That is the course I pursued and have never regretted. Immediately after graduating from high school, I entered Central Business College in Denver. Skills such as taking shorthand and operating a PBX machine are useless now, but how could anyone have foreseen the importance of learning to type? I graduated in 1966 at the age of 19 and was given a job with Central Business College – and I married Larry. I worked for the school for several years. Throughout this time I was taking art courses at every opportunity.

Meininger Art Supply store in downtown Denver displayed a magnificent painting by James Disney. *Aspen Flowers* was an exquisitely detailed aspen grove. It stopped me in my tracks, and he was teaching art! Jim was a mountain climber and outstanding painter. His method of teaching was to mix three distinct values – light, medium, and dark. While this approach was overly simplified, it did launch me in the right direction.

When I married Joe Branney in 1973, I became an instant mom to Scott, age 13, John, age 12, and Sean age 6. The boys are posing with my collie Sammy.

Veryl feeding Andy, the one legged- goose

We had a large pond in Englewood, Colorado. As a gosling, Andy had his leg bitten off by a snapping turtle. He was rescued and given to me to raise. Andy was terribly handicapped without his leg, and I straddled him for two years, protecting him from the other geese on our pond at feeding time. He felt safest in my studio modeling

I was too young to appreciate Larry's unwavering support of my artistic goals, and our marriage didn't last. During the years after our brief marriage, I was relentless in pursuing an art education. Denver had and still has a nucleus of great artists who pursue realism. Ned Jacob directed me to life drawing classes and to *Carlson's Guide to Landscape Painting* by John F. Carlson. Even today this book is like a bible to representational artists. I have a hardback copy of his book with a $5.95 price penciled on the inside cover.

Like many realistic artists of my generation, I set out to learn the technical skills from any available source. I keenly felt a need to better understand anatomy to be more convincing with my work. The painter I admired the most was Carl Rungius. He hunted his models and then drew from the carcasses. This would never work for me. Loving animals was my inspiration. I could never destroy an animal to create it in art.

I met Ken Bunn about this time and was awed by his sculpture. I immediately saw sculpture as a way to learn anatomy. Ken set me up with my first armature, a pipe attached to a board with a tee at the top through which to run supporting wires. My Dad later "improved" the armature by adding a coupling to the supportive pipe. This way I had two pipes and could adjust the height of my subject from the work board.

It is interesting that as much as I loved horses, I was pursuing wildlife painting. Somewhere in the back of my mind was the idea that I couldn't possibly make a living portraying the animal I loved the most, the horse.

President Nixon signed The Endangered Species Act on December 28, 1973. This had a powerful influence on many artists then and now. Conservation-related stories were frequently in the news. Using art to benefit animals was certainly in line with my heart.

During the 1970's and well into the 1980's, the wildlife art market was largely confined to creating big game animals for hunters. The acceptance of art portraying non-game species, as well as females and young, was heavily influenced with the creation of the National Museum of Wildlife Art in Jackson, Wyoming, 1987. The museum's founders, Bill and Joffa Kerr, have contributed substantially to encouraging a broader portrayal of all wildlife through permanent exhibits, as well at during the annual Western Visions miniature show.

I met trial attorney Joe Branney in 1972. I took his name and number as a potential collector. Joe had hunted all over North America and indicated an interest in purchasing my work. By the time I contacted Joe, he was divorced and raising his three sons. Our dates were to the Denver Zoo to watch the bull elk bugling and into Waterton Canyon west of Denver to see bighorn sheep in the wild.

Preening, 1978, 8 x 9 x 9 inches

Greenwing Teal Drakes, 1986, 12 x 14 x 2 inches

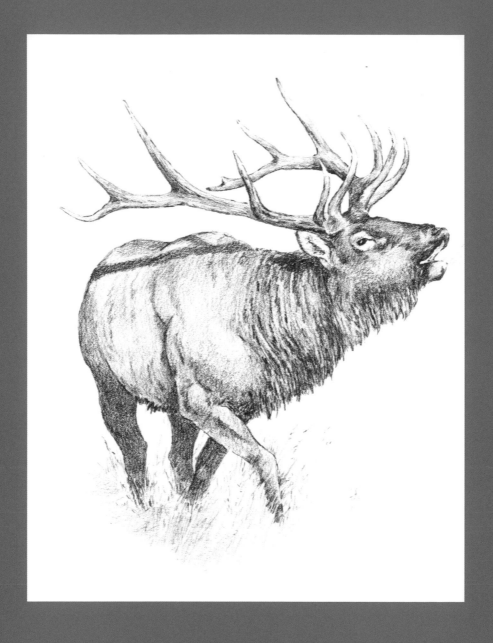

An Echo in the Next Clearing, 1977, 20 x 32 inches

The Bluff, 1979, 15 x 19 x 9 inches

Gold Medal for Sculpture 1979
Wildlife Artists International

Watching bears on the McNeil River in Alaska, 1974

Photographing in British Columbia

Joe rode horses and had a barn and he wanted horses again. He was interested in everything I was interested in. We were married three months after our first date. I became a step mom to three boys, Sean, John and Scott aged 6, 12, and 13. Joe and my father turned the barn loft into my first great studio.

During the ten years Joe and I were together, our lives revolved around the cycles of wildlife. Joe put down his guns in deference to my love of animals and became an outstanding wildlife photographer. We were in Yellowstone every fall to photograph the rut of the elk and pursued every wildlife photo opportunity along the back bone of the Rocky Mountains.

We "grand slammed" on film. This is a hunting term for having "bagged" all four of the North American wild sheep. We photographed Bighorns in Colorado and Wyoming, Dall sheep in Alaska, Stone Sheep in Canada, and Desert Bighorns in Nevada. Our adventures took us into Alaska onto the McNeil River to see the Kodiak Bears and onto Round Island to see the Walrus. We had a pond at our home, and I raised several species of waterfowl while sculpting ducks to benefit Ducks Unlimited.

Initially I was torn between wildlife painting and the new challenges of sculpture. My first sculpture, a bighorn ram, was cast in an edition of 10 and sold out immediately. This encouraged me to sculpt more of the subjects that were constantly in my camera lens. Sculpting, however, seemed to require more precision and understanding of the subjects than photography alone provided. I discovered that while painting is an illusion, sculpture was reality. I had to understand the subjects not just from a 360-degree vantage point but from the top and underneath as well. Understanding anatomy was the key to the treasure chest of creativity.

Jon Zahourek, one of the talented artists in Denver's artist community, was teaching in-depth courses on horse and human anatomy. Jon created very accurate scaled down resin skeletons called the Equiniken and the Maniken. He takes every single muscle of the horse and the human and teaches the principles of origin and insertion and the functions of each muscle by sculpting clay muscles onto the skeletons. This was the breakthrough I needed, and these courses gave me the key I was searching for. I took both the human and horse courses twice.

Promenade, 1979, 22 x 14 x 12 inches

On the Crest of a Wave, 1980, 24 x 22 x 19 inches (45 inch wingspan)

Veryl with Cody. Cody belonged to
Dr. Gregory Hayes in Boulder, Colorado and
was used in movie work.

Jon's work with artists helped improve the work of an entire generation of representational artists growing up in what was otherwise an
abstract world. Jon Zahourek's Equinken class not only gave me the
desired knowledge of anatomy, it reconnected me artistically with the
animal I love the most – the horse.

Wildlife sculptor Ken Bunn helped initiate what is now a thriving
sculpture community in Loveland, Colorado. In 1972 Bob Zimmerman
converted an industrial foundry to a fine art bronze foundry at the urging
of Ken and Fritz White. I was fortunate to begin a career during the
early years of Art Castings of Colorado. One day a week I would drive
from Denver to Loveland to work on waxes, approve the metal chasing
and oversee the patinas on my sculptures. Several of today's best-known
American sculptors began their careers in Loveland during the 1970's.
Bob was casting work for George Lundeen, Ken Bunn, George Carlson,
Fritz White, Glenna Goodacre, Kent Ullberg, Gerald Balciar, Dan Oster-
miller and myself.

Thus the Denver group of artists, particularly Ken Bunn, Ned Jacob,
and Jon Zahourek, were powerful influences on my early years. I
continue to admire them for their work and artistic integrity. In 2006 I
took a horse painting workshop with Ned in Scottsdale. Never an artist
to bypass challenges, Ned had us painting saddled appaloosa horses from
life by the end of the week.

Hunter Along the Rimrock, 1980, 19 x 22 x 8 inches

Old Maude

Charles Goodnight invented the chuckwagon as a means to feed the cowboys during the long cattle drives of the 1860's. Julius Roberts, a Walsenburg rancher, restored this chuckwagon and drove his mules along part of the original Goodnight Trail during the 1982 re-enactment.

I am only distantly related to Charles Goodnight, but having the last name of Goodnight has influenced my artwork and interests throughout life. Charles and Mary Ann Goodnight did not have children, so there are no direct descendants.

It wasn't until in high school that I learned I was adopted by Dale Goodnight when he married my Mom. I was 1 1/2 years old, and Dale is the only father I have ever known. He can be traced back to Christian Gutknecht who emigrated from Germany, landing in Germantown, Pennsylvania in 1749. Colonel Charles Goodnight can be traced back to Christian's brother, George, who emigrated in 1754. George, and a third brother, John Michael, changed their last names from Gutknecht to the English translation of Goodnight upon arriving in America. Christian retained the Gutknecht surname and only spoke German throughout his lifetime, however his childen were given the surname of Goodnight. Thus began the history of the Goodnight family in America.

In the late 1970's, I had a surprise visit from Evetts Haley, Jr. Evetts' father; Evetts Haley, Sr. was the author of *Charles Goodnight – Cowman and Plainsman*.

The Haley Memorial Library in Midland, Texas wanted a life-sized sculpture of Old Maude, a favorite longhorn cow that Goodnight says had "29 calves by actual count." I had not yet done a life-sized sculpture and was initially intimidated by the proposition. After overcoming the fear, however, I visited the Haley Ranch in Sallisaw, Oklahoma. While there, I was fortunate enough to actually see a longhorn calf born. The working model of Old Maude was created from this experience.

During the process of creating this sculpture, I met Stan Searle, a longhorn rancher and publisher of the Texas Longhorn Journal. Stan's own longhorns were in Southern Colorado not far from where the Goodnight/Loving Trail entered Colorado. Stan organized a few of his neigh-

Veryl's research of the longhorn began in April 1980, when she visited the J. Evetts Haley Ranch near Sallisaw, Oklahoma to observe cattle during the calving season. The sketches, photographs and notes from that visit served as a basis for Veryl's composition of "Old Maude," the range-grizzled survivor with yet another calf to nurse. Excerpt from "Old Maude" booklet published by the Haley Memorial Library, Midland, Texas.

bors to stage a mock cattle drive. An old chuck wagon was restored and hooked to a team of mules for the drive. We rode along 25 miles of the trail that had not changed since 1866 when Goodnight took the cattle over.

Evetts Haley, Senior, came along under the condition he could be the camp cook. He brought his own sourdough starter and steaks, not trusting anyone else to create an authentic trail meal. My father came as well. Robert Carr Vincent and his son Carr Vincent, ranchers and board members of the Haley Library, helped keep the cattle in line. And Jim Haley, a cowboy to the core, and grandson of Evetts Haley also came. The drive was only 25 miles, and we were only out one night, but it was a life changing experience.

J. Evetts Haley, Sr., Dale Goodnight, and Don Johnston during the 1982 longhorn drive re-enactment.

Trail Wise by Wendy Shattil

Old Maude, 1982
Haley Memorial Library

The Goodnights and Art by B. Byron Price

Charles Goodnight with his bison Old Sikes. Photograph courtesy of the Nita Stewart Haley Memorial Library, Midland, Texas.

Just a few months before his death in December, 1929, Charles Goodnight sat impatiently in the studio of William Herbert "Buck" Dunton, at Taos, New Mexico, while the artist rendered his portrait. The aged rancher had answered the artist's summons reluctantly, bellowing that there were "more pictures of Goodnight in Texas than buzzards, and just about as useful." Although this was surely a self deprecating exaggeration, the old man *had* posed for many photographers over the years and his distinctive countenance *had* graced the pages of magazines and newspapers in the Lone Star State and elsewhere in the nation on more than one occasion. Regardless, Goodnight's pose for Dunton was brief, just long enough for a quick sketch before departing without ever bothering to appraise the result.

Goodnight's biographer, J. Evetts Haley, who had accompanied the still vigorous ninety-three year old to Taos, surmised that the cowman had difficulty sitting still long enough for an artist to capture his likeness. A renowned frontiersman, trail driver and livestock breeder, Charles Goodnight was always a man of action, pursuing his business interests with a single-minded devotion that left little time for art and culture. Although he had once been part-owner of a Pueblo, Colorado, opera house, Goodnight's main interests were economic and scientific and, living most of his life on the remote grasslands of western Texas, artists seldom cut his trail.

The cattle business prompted Goodnight's first recorded brush with an artist in 1886, when he engaged John C. Cowles, an itinerant landscape painter and student of the famed American artist, Albert Bierstadt, to paint two large canvases of famed JA ranch in the Texas Panhandle. Cowles spent the summer on the JA sketching, painting and gathering information on the ranch in hopes that the finished products would help Goodnight and his business partner Cornelia Adair sell the ranch. Adair's husband, John, a prominent investment broker from Ireland, had died the previous year, just as the bottom had fallen out of the cattle market. Farmers were beginning to flood into the Panhandle and, pessimistic about the future of large-scale cattle ranching there, Goodnight had given Cowles's brother Egbert, a Minneapolis, Minnesota, banker, an option to find a buyer for the ranch.

According to Goodnight, Albert Bierstadt himself eventually became involved in the effort to find a purchaser for the JA, although to no avail. Eventually the partners divided the ranch's assets, overcame the difficulties of the moment and continued to pursue the cattle business independently.

Goodnight retained the Cowles paintings, which were produced at his expense, and eventually hung them in the new home that he and his wife Mary, called Molly by her friends, built on a new 160 section ranch they acquired north of the JA, near the Fort Worth and Denver railroad in Armstrong County. The few scant descriptions that exist of the interior of the 2,900 square foot, Victorian structure fail to mention other art works that the Goodnights may have owned. Several visitors did, however, recall leaded stain glass windows and walls adorned with an abundance of framed photographs, firearms and Indian artifacts, most of the latter dating from Goodnight's days as a scout and ranger.

After leaving the JA Ranch in 1887, Goodnight continued to enjoy success in raising and marketing high grade Hereford cattle, often in partnership with others. As the years passed, however, land speculation and ill-advised investments in meat packing and Mexican silver mining whittled away his fortune.

Increasingly, his interests turned to the cross-breeding of cattle with a herd of bison that also grazed his pastures. The Panhandle had teamed with the shaggy beasts when the Goodnights had arrived in the region in the mid-1870s, but most had been hunted out to make way for livestock. Alarmed by the relentless slaughter and fearful that the species might disappear forever, Mary Goodnight, in 1878, encouraged her husband to capture several orphan calves to raise as pets.

By 1894, the Goodnight ranch was home to more than twenty-five bison, one of the largest herds in the United States. These purebreds were joined by an equal number of mixed-blood "cattalos", created by the crossing of bison with Polled Angus or Galloway cattle. From the early 1890s onward Goodnight continually experimented with such crosses in hopes of producing a profitable hybrid that combined the best qualities of both species.

At Mary's insistence, Goodnight eventually set aside a separate 600 acre pasture for the bison, which had formerly shared the range with a variety of other indigenous

and imported species, including quail, wild turkey, antelope, deer, elk and, briefly, even a moose. In time, Goodnight's intense interest in animal genetics led him to purchase hogs and imported Karakul sheep as well.

The bison and cattalo herd grew steadily and was trimmed annually through slaughter and sale. The Goodnights actively marketed bison meat, hides, horns and head mounts to customers throughout the county and sold live animals to other ranchers and to zoos in such cities as San Antonio, Denver, New York and Munich. Yellowstone National Park also purchased several Goodnight bison as did entertainer William F. Cody, who featured them in Buffalo Bill's Wild West show.

During World War I, the couple donated a bison that was sold for the relief of suffering Belgians. Not long after they sent General John J. Pershing, the commander of the American Expeditionary Force to Europe, a pair of bison wool socks, for which the officer expressed his warm appreciation. Goodnight's periodic gifts of bison meat, hides, tallow and calves and occasional invitations to hunt on his ranch, endeared him to members of the Kiowa, Comanche and Pueblo tribes.

Goodnight joined the American Bison Society in 1908 and was an active member until his death. Although a tireless promoter of bison hybrids and byproducts for more than three decades, his dream of producing a commercially viable bison-cattle cross-breed went unfulfilled. Nor did he achieve his goal of turning his ranch into a government park or game preserve. His widely disseminated observations and ideas about animal genetics brought him considerable public acclaim, nevertheless, and earned him the sobriquet, "The Luther Burbank of the Range."

Ironically, Molly Goodnight actually owned the bison herd that made her husband famous and it was she who encouraged his first efforts at cross-breeding the species with cattle. She never sought the spotlight, however, and it only rarely shined her way. Yet to those who knew her best, Molly was a steadfast friend and neighbor. She had endured isolation and hardship without becoming coarse, had ministered to the sick and held church services in her home when the need arose, and although she had no children of her own, had been a mother to her younger siblings, the cowboys who worked for her husband and the students of nearby Goodnight College, a local school the couple established in 1898.

Charles Goodnight survived the death of his devoted wife by three years. In 1928, admirers in the city of Amarillo began a fund drive to commission an oil portrait of the man, who many now called the "Father of the Texas Panhandle." Goodnight reluctantly agreed, provided the artist was a "Panhandle product." Historian J. Evetts Haley convinced Goodnight that Harold Bugbee, a budding Clarendon, Texas, artist and rancher was the right person for the job. He was, and would later illustrate Haley's masterful biography *Charles Goodnight, Cowman and Plainsman*.

Other artists inspired by Charles Goodnight's example, have, in the eighty years since his passing, continued to render his likeness, capture his character and immortalize his colorful deeds in paint and bronze. Until recently, Molly Goodnight has been overshadowed in art, as in life, by her husband's larger than life persona. Over the past decade, however, her remarkable story has been rediscovered and interpreted anew by artist Veryl Goodnight. Possessing more than a genealogist's interest in her family lineage, Veryl has interpreted aspects of Molly Goodnight's intriguing and inspiring life experience with skill and imagination in such sculptures as *Back from the Brink* and *The Gathering*. These sensitive and poetic portrayals in bronze reflect not only the solace and companionship that Molly found in nature and the critical role she played in the preservation of one of its endangered creatures but also reveal much about the sculptor's own deep and abiding love of natural world.

Byron Price holds the Charles Marion Russell Memorial Chair and is Director of Charles M. Russell Center for the Study of Art of the American West at the University of Oklahoma and is Director of the University of Oklahoma Press. He is a 1970 graduate of the United States Military Academy at West Point and earned an MA in Museum Science at Texas Tech University in 1977. Before taking his current position, Price spent nearly 25 years in the museum profession, serving as executive director of the Panhandle Plains Historical Museum in Canyon, Texas; the National Cowboy Hall of Fame and Western Heritage Center in Oklahoma City; and the Buffalo Bill Historical Center in Cody, Wyoming. Price is the author of more than three dozen journal articles on western American history and art and has written several books including Fine Art of the West (2004); The Chuck Wagon Cook Book (2004); Erwin E. Smith: Cowboy Photographer (1997); and Cowboys of the American West (1996). He is also the editor of the award-winning Charles M. Russell: A Catalogue Raisonné (2007).

In 1887 Charles Goodnight built Mary Ann this Victorian home on the edge of the Palo Duro Canyon in Armstrong Country. This grand old home on the Pandhandle of Texas is being restored to become The Charles Goodnight Historical Center.

Northwest Rendezvous

Robert Bateman, Veryl, Jessica Zemsky, and Jack Hines

Phil Whitehawk and his wife, Connie Bellet, were two of the re-enactors during the early NWR Paint Outs. Phil's music influenced several of Veryl's sculptures, including *Wither Deep In Powder*.

In addition to the cattle drive, an invitation to participate in the Northwest Rendezvous art show added to my growing interest in portraying history as well as wildlife and domestic animals. In 1980 I was invited to be a guest artist at the annual Northwest Rendezvous show held in Helena, Montana. The show was preceded by a Paint Out. The camp was located on the Madison River outside of West Yellowstone, Montana. Gary Carter was part of the group at that time, and he arranged to have authentically-attired mountain men and women present for us to draw and paint. This was a stimulating experience to work along side outstanding artists such as Gary Carter, Ray Swanson, Paul Calle, Hollis Williford, Jack Hines and Jessica Zemensky. I was out of my comfort zone doing figurative work, so I hauled a donkey over to the camp from a neighboring ranch. However, I soon found myself caught up in the obsessive work habits of the other artists present and joined them in drawing whatever and whoever were in a line of sight. We worked late into the night sketching by firelight.

It was during this camp that I attempted my first figurative sculpture, a portrait of Ed Keney, one of the mountain men re-enactors. Ed lived the history, actually spending Montana winters in a teepee. While I was sculpting him, he spoke of his "symphony being the sound of geese flying north" and "his tiffany glass was the frost on the windowpane each winter."

Re-enactors Phil Whitehawk and his wife Connie Bellet, did multimedia presentations in the evenings combining Phil's historically rich lyrics with Connie's photography of the mountains and wildlife of Montana. I was captured by the musical vision of times gone by and of the eagle soaring overhead and the White Buffalo battling a blizzard.

These visions gave me a much-needed new perspective. My beautiful home in Cherry Hills Village lost its importance. The boys – Scott, John, and Sean – were raised. My relationship with Joe was increasingly contentious, and it was time to move on.

I still show annually with NWR, and the artist members are some of my oldest and dearest friends. The group has grown and flourished over the years under the guidance of our President, Frank Montibeller. Newer members, particularly Tom Saubert, have stepped in and taken on the tasks of organizing the annual Paint Out. NWR is now partners with The Montana Historical Society, and exciting events during the show, such

Wither Deep In Powder (stainless steel), 1982, 16 x 22 x 8 inches

as the Saturday morning Quick Draw, are supported through the efforts of dozens of volunteers. Devoted collectors of NWR artists flock to Helena every August. In 2010, I took Emeritus membership status; however, I plan to continue to participate as much as possible for as long as is possible. NWR is my "Heart Show".

"As the days grow shorter each fall, it triggers an instinct in the elk to migrate from the high ranges to the open meadows below. In the gray predawn you can see a white sheet of frost on the backs of the bulls, and their breath hangs in clouds as they bugle their challenges. The ritual lasts only a few weeks and is filled with a sense of urgency — the spirit of autumn."

Spirit of Autumn, 1984, 16 x 24 x 12 inches

Fall Buck, etching, 1989, 5 x 7 inches

Fall Does, etching, 1989, 5 x 7 inches

Maude II, etching, 1989, 5 x 7 inches

Siesta, etching, 1989, 5 x 7 inches

Pronghorns (Drawing), 1973, 17 x 27 inches

Castle Rock, Colorado
(1982–1987)

The call of history and the lure of the mountains led me to a log home just south of Denver and west of Castle Rock, Colorado. I was rebuilding my life to balance today's reality with a wish to have lived in a different time. Part of this reality included a bronze finishing foundry which I located on the lower level of the log home.

While doing some limited casting at a small foundry in Denver, I met Dimitry Spiridon. Dimitry had arrived in the United States as a political refugee from Communist Romania. He was learning the foundry business from a fellow Romanian. I hired Dimitry in 1985, and he has done the metal chasing and patinas on my work ever since.

My Castle Rock years were productive, and it was here that I fully realized the importance of working from life. My studio was again a barn conversion, and I installed a sliding glass door between a stall and the studio as well as a high chain link fence to the south to contain various models. I had a wildlife rehabilitation license and raised two mule deer fawns, a coyote pup and Petie, a prairie dog who had been left on the steps of the Denver Zoo. I also kept a blind cow elk for Colorado State University, using her as a model in *Spirit of Autumn*.

It was in Castle Rock that I created the first two Western Women sculptures of a continuing series. I suppose I envision myself as a pioneer woman, living close to the land and sharing my life with animals. The animal/human relationship was always important to me. The first attempt and to this day one of the most successful was "Cares for Her Brothers."

I had an art show in Fort Collins with Ben Nighthorse Campbell, a Northern Cheyenne. On the way back to his home in Ignacio, Colorado, he stopped to visit. He came at feeding time and had to follow me around from animal to animal. A few weeks later I received a beaded necklace and a letter from Ben. It stated, "I told my Grandmother of a woman whose heart goes out to all living things. She said she should be known as Ewu Wumishi HeMe – Cares for Her Brothers." I chose to portray this honorable name through a sculpture of a pioneer women cradling an abandoned fawn deer.

I raised two orphan fawns for the Colorado Game and Fish Department and used them as models to create this sculpture. Wumishi simply disappeared one overcast day, I always hoped she joined the local herd.

Dimitry Spiridon working on *Cares For Her Brothers*

Wumishi

Cares for Her Brothers, 1985, 34 x 38 x 32 inches

Melody contracted a lung disease and died in my arms after the vet exhausted all efforts to save her.

A life-sized casting of *Cares for Her Brothers* was installed in the Denver Zoo. In 1987 another casting was placed in the prestigious Brookgreen Gardens in South Carolina. Brookgreen has the largest collection of American sculpture in the world. It was founded by one of my heroes, Anna Hyatt Huntington, and her husband, Archer Huntington, in 1931.

Cares at Brookgreen by Anna Malarich

Cares for Her Brothers
Brookgreen Gardens, near Myrtle Beach, South Carolina was established in 1931 by Archer and Anna Hyatt Huntington.
It has the largest collection of American Sculpture in the world.

Thoughts on *Cares for Her Brothers* at Brookgreen Gardens

It's one of those artworks that demands attention – not in a loud or offensive way, but in a manner that compels the viewer to come closer. The mystique of *Cares for Her Brothers* was evident from the time it was placed at Brookgreen Gardens in 1987. Through the years, our staff and volunteers have declared it to be a favorite and our visitors have wanted to linger near it. I am aware of the ashes of at least three persons that have been scattered around her base. The last scattering included the ashes of the conservation volunteer who cared for *Cares*, ensuring that his final resting place was near the sculpture he loved.

The woman's face, hands, knee, foot, and apron bear the mark of the public's attention. This does not detract from the figure; rather, it underscores her humanity. The light discolorations have been rendered by loving touches, even caresses, from the hands of many visitors as they appreciate the figure's beauty, compassion, and strength, and the meaning of her Native American name. There are many important sculptures in the Brookgreen collection, but only a few have that kind of magic.

Robin R. Salmon
Vice President for Collections and Curator of Sculpture
Brookgreen Gardens

Celebration of Spring, 1984, 11 x 6 x 4 inches

Common Goals (detail), 1986, 22 x 15 x 10 inches

Roger

The opportunity to seriously pursue my lifetime love of horses also blossomed while living in Castle Rock. I had purchased the horse of my dreams in 1976. After buying and selling several horses, a white Arabian named Gwalowa became my partner for the next twenty years. Gwalowa taught me to ride and he taught me to sculpt.

I rode Gwalowa in fifty mile endurance races; he was my partner in a sport called "Ride and Tie." He worked cattle on the Goodnight Trail re-enactment and I rode him in English tack with the Arapahoe Hunt Club. During this time I began teaching horse sculpture, and Gwalowa was my partner there as well.

Gwalowa

And it was on Gwalowa's back in 1987, that I met my partner in life, Roger Brooks.

I was riding Gwalowa on private land just west of Castle Rock, when another rider appeared on a ridgeline. Gwalowa was a full-blooded Arabian and stood only 14.3 hands tall. Roger was riding his 17.2 hand tall warm blood, Kepler. All I could say when we got within hearing distance was "I have never been on a horse that tall!" Roger's reply was "I have never been on one that short." We traded horses.

Roger was three years older than me and had never been married. He was born in Orinda, California, but had been raised primarily in Scottsdale, Arizona. He graduated from Arizona State University with a degree in business, but didn't want a lifetime of deskwork, so he took flying lessons. In 1968 and 1969 he hired on as the youngest pilot to fly covert CIA missions for Air America in Laos. After living abroad for a few years, he returned to the United States to begin a career as a professional airline pilot. He was with Frontier Airlines from 1973 and was flying as a Captain when Frontier merged with Continental Airlines in 1986. When we met, Roger was unhappily flying for Continental and he was simultaneously managing legal cases on behalf of the Frontier pilots. Roger lived alone in Aurora, on the east side of Denver, with a cat named Ace. His horse Kepler was boarded just three miles from my Castle Rock home.

Roger on Kepler

Our initial dates were quite amusing. Roger was the typical confirmed bachelor and only came to my home out of curiosity about my pet prairie dog, Petie. Petie had just come into puberty and I was part of his family group known as a "coterie." Roger was definitely not welcome as far as Petie was concerned. The two-pound prairie dog won more than one battle with the 225-pound pilot. In spite of loosing a good deal of blood to Petie, Roger helped devise an elaborate release system to help integrate Petie into a nearby prairie dog colony.

Roger not only rode a beautiful horse – we shared the same respect for animals.

Dawn In Dog City, 1988, 8 x 10 x 8 inches

Morning Dew, 1986, 6 x 12 x 5 inches

The Newcomer, 1984, 9 x 9 x 6 inches

The Lesson, 1986, 7 x 16 x 8 inches

The Release by Wendy Shattil

Dr. Gregory Hayes asked if I would be interested in raising Calamity and imprinting her for future movie work. Her mother was getting old and Dr. Hayes needed a replacement. I kept her with me night and day, but she was not of the same temperament as her mother.

After careful planning, Calamity was released in a safe location where other riders could gradually wean her from human assistance.

Absolutely the only time Calamity displayed affection was when she returned, as if to thank me for setting her free.

THE LESSON

Calamity taught me well
Taught me the essence of a Coyote
Keen yellow eyes told me
That neither leash nor love
Could make her what she wasn't

With a sympathetic heart
I thanked her for the lesson
I took her where she yearned to be
Gave her back her birthright
Set her free

by Veryl Goodnight

Paint Mare & Filly and Team Ropers

I completed two additional large sculptures in the Castle Rock studio. The first was the life-sized *Paint Mare and Filly*, which was installed in 1986 at the National Cowboy and Western Heritage Museum in Oklahoma City. The second was *Team Ropers*, a 1 1/2 life-sized portrayal of a young cowboy playing with his border collie. This sculpture was commissioned as the entrance art for Stroh Ranch in Franktown, Colorado.

These two monuments gave Roger and me our first adventures together in the art world. I had a rickety two-wheeled flat bed on which to haul the 1,700 pound *Paint Mare and Filly* from Colorado to the Cowboy Hall of Fame. Roger was very safety-conscious and took a leave of absence from his flight schedule to make sure that his new girlfriend and her precious cargo made it to Oklahoma City in one piece. Once in Oklahoma City, he found himself directing the crane operator and assisting in the installation of the bronze. He repeated these tasks just a few months later when installing *Team Ropers* in Franktown.

The first casting of Team Ropers was installed in 1988 at Stroh Ranch in Parker, Colorado. This portrayal of a bond between a boy and his dog was also selected in 1991 for the permanent collection of art at the Houston Astrodome and for the Pro Rodeo Hall of Fame in Colorado Springs, Colorado.

Paint Mare and Filly, 1985
National Cowboy and Western
Heritage Museum
Oklahoma City, Oklahoma

Paint Filly, 1985, 7 x 8 x 4 inches

Paint Mare and Filly, 1985, 17 x 21 x 8 inches

*Team Ropers
Clay*, 1985
Veryl and
model, Justin
Brazell, with the
completed clay
sculpture

After the Hunt, 1988, 19 x 18 x 15 inches

Both Roger and I "Rode to the Hounds" and have our "buttons" with the Arapahoe Hunt in Colorado. George Beeman was huntsman for 55 years and has left three generations of horseman following his extraordinary example.

Unlike the image of most Hunt clubs, killing was not the goal of the Arapahoe Hunt, or I could not have been a participant. We rode after coyotes, which never failed to outwit and out-run the hounds and riders.

BEYOND TRADITION

Tradition begins early
    For the field
        Tying stocks and pulling on black shiny boots
          But for one
It begins pre-dawn
    Readying the horses and hounds
        Brushing and feeding and patting each one
The field is gathered
    On bays and grays
        Wearing scarlet and black and well polished tack
Each takes a place
    Behind the man and his hounds
        As the snow falls softly
          Collecting on their shoulders and hats
The only sounds
    Are oak brush scraping leather
        And impatient knickers
        Then the stillness is broken
By the baying of hounds and blast of the horn
    And we are racing wildly after a quarry
        That we seldom see and don't want to catch

The field's day is now complete
    As we head back to the barn
        Looking like apparitions
          In the rising steam from our mounts
The warmth of the fire and the brandy
    Will soon feel good
        To all but one
The hounds will be gathered
    For the slow walk home
        Brandy and fire don't cross his mind
          As his tradition doesn't end with the last run
His horse and hounds worked hard
    And the day is not complete
        Until he has thanked each and every one

by Veryl Goodnight

PART TWO

New Mexico

1987-2006

Veryl sculpting the "Freedom Horses" in her Santa Fe studio

Santa Fe

I was forty years old in 1987, single, and had lived in Colorado my entire life. My work was beginning to receive national recognition, and I felt a need to move to a more vibrant artistic community, Santa Fe.

My father died unexpectedly on December 3, 1985. Two weeks earlier he had replaced a corral gate for me. I had no reason to believe he would not live forever. My Mom had been ill with lung cancer for a very long time. Her death was imminent, but not my father's. Four months later, on March 17, 1986, Mom also died. The death of my parents was the final catalyst to relocate.

Then I met Roger. This was an unexpected twist. He asked me to explain my reasons for relocating. He visited Santa Fe with me. After a great deal of probing and exploring consequences I had not even considered, Roger endorsed my decision. This was not the end of our relationship, but the true beginning. As an airline pilot, he could fly anywhere for free. To commute from Denver to Albuquerque was routine for him.

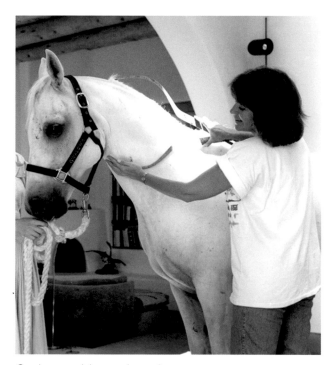

Gwalowa modeling on the studio stage

Roger was extremely helpful in making the transition from Colorado to Santa Fe. During the process, he became increasingly involved in the business of my career, utilizing his business degree from Arizona State University. He continued to prolong his "leave of absence" from Continental Airlines.

We found land north of Santa Fe just outside Tesuque adjoining the historic resort Rancho Encantado. I boarded my horses, donkey and "Little Joe the Wrangler" – a pygmy goat – at Rancho Encantado. The riding was new and exciting. There were miles of galloping in the wide sandy arroyos before ascending the ridge lines with endless views. Roger would often drive down and bring Kepler to explore this new country. Horses are easy to move, but when he finally brought his cat, Ace, I knew he was committed.

I rented a house on Palace Avenue and a temporary office/studio at Sena Plaza in the heart of old Santa Fe. The newness of Santa Fe was exhilarating. The warm glow off the adobe walls overcame the grayness of the infrequent overcast days. The old wooden gates with peeling paint, the uneven wooden vigas jutting out of the adobe "portals," and the leaning "coyote fencing" gave New Mexico an old world feeling.

We were walking distance from both Canyon Road and to the newly rented studio at Sena Plaza. Santa Fe was full of galleries. Western tra-

Spring and Sprite, 1999, 8 feet x 10 feet x 2 feet 4 inches

Spring and Sprite is located in several private collections as well as at the Old West Museum in Cheyenne, Wyoming and the in the town of Westcliffe, Colorado. The last casting in the edition, shown in this photo, was unveiled in Woodside, California August 31, 2010.

ditional art was interspersed with art of every possible description. I became more accepting of non-representational artistic visions.

The Sena Plaza studio was upstairs next to the offices of Cricket and Gordon Heiss, who managed La Casa Sena Restaurant and Cantina. The charming old building was built in 1848 and was originally the home of General Sena. My studio had a large north window, uneven wooden floor, plaster walls, and a dark ceiling of wood and vigas. It had served as a studio to other artists before me. Downstairs, the elegant restaurant and cantina became a social center for Roger and me. Many evenings were spent with the Heiss family listening to the talented waiters sing hits from Broadway plays such as *Phantom of the Opera*. Santa Fe is totally about art, whether it was a food presentation, architecture, gardening, music, or writing.

Stormy, 2006, 11 x 18 x 5 inches

I met Sharon Woods, author of *Santa Fe Style*, and owner of Woods Construction. Sharon and I hit it off immediately, and together we began to plan a small home and dream studio for the eleven acres in Tesuque. Designing an architecturally compatible and functional barn was very important. A barn not only houses my animals but is an extension of the studio.

The charm of living "in town" wore off quickly. I wanted to be out – away from the street noise and barking dogs and close to my horses just as soon as possible.

Roger and I moved into the tiny casita behind the new large studio in the spring of 1989. We had built with a contingency plan. The casita was ideal for a single woman should things "not work out for us." If they did, we could eventually build a larger home up on the hill to the south.

Even though Roger was maintaining an "exit strategy," he sold his properties in Denver and put his money into our building project. Late in the afternoon of Christmas Eve, 1989, we walked over the hill to Rancho Encantado and brought Gwalowa, Kepler and Dancer home to their new barn. Later that evening, Roger asked me to marry him. His proposal was carefully written on a tiny piece of paper in a silver heart shaped locket. It was under a can of cat food in my Christmas Stocking. After laughing over the can of cat food, I said yes to sharing our lives forever.

Stormy (detail), 2006, 11 x 18 x 5 inches

Running the Chaparral (detail), 1997, 27 x 27 x 17 inches

The Sculpture Garden

Living in the desert southwest had many advantages and many adjustments. While the architecture was visually exciting, the surrounding landscape felt barren. I was driven to build an oasis of aspens and wildflowers around the studio. A waterfall and koi pond was in the center of the winding paths, lined with stucco sculpture stands.

Many of the people who visited Santa Fe came to seek out art and artists. Several touring companies brought large groups to the studio and garden. The sculpture garden also attracted the most important patrons of my career; Bill and Sue Keck, Joe and Betty Moore, Take Miyama, John Koontz, John and Saralynne Geraghty, and John and Sarah Lindahl.

Iris Garden, 1997, 12 x 10 x 6 inches

The Newcomer, Life-size, 1991, 34 x 34 x 15 inches

What Friends Are For, 1988, 9 x 15 x 8 inches

The first sculpture completed in Santa Fe was of my beloved horse Gwalowa and his burro friend, Burrito. *What Friends Are For* portrays two friends leaning on each other. I placed them in their new environment, inspired by the rhythm of the twisting arroyos and chamisa.

Rivalry, 2005, 24 x 30 x 12 inches

Houdini

Houdini shortly before her release. She had reduced her winter "den," a large wooden crate to toothpicks as her message that she was ready to be released.

The barn was nearing completion in late October, when we received a call asking if we could house a black bear cub for the winter. I had secured a New Mexico Wildlife Rehabilitation license right after moving to Santa Fe. The New Mexico Game and Fish had no place to winter a bear cub that was found the night before in a tree next to the St. Francis Cathedral in downtown Santa Fe. The bear cub had apparently been separated from her mother as the two searched for food.

Additional chicken wire was quickly added to close in the open space between the top of the stalls and the ceiling. We put a crate in one corner and filled that corner with pine boughs to give her a place to hide, and the half starved cub was placed in a large steel sided stall of our unfinished barn.

Three nights later she disappeared. She had managed to climb the bars on the upper half of the stall and had pushed out through the chicken wire where it joined the wall. We were only a half-mile from the National Forest, but she made it 10 miles back to the heart of Santa Fe where she was originally captured. This time she was found on top of a power pole. Santa Fe immediately turned out all electricity to that part of town, not wanting the bad publicity that Albuquerque had a month earlier. This had been a notoriously dry year, and bears were coming into towns for food. The Albuquerque bear was tranquilized when found on a power pole. She fell into the power lines, sending sparks flying, and seriously burning herself. The photos of the burned bear shot around the world. Santa Fe opted to have half the town late to work rather than risk harming their bear.

The chicken wire was reinforced, and the cub, now named Houdini, settled in for a winter of good food that came from some of Santa Fe's best restaurants. Houdini was to be kept wild. No problem. She was already more than six months old when captured, and her instincts were intact. I would slip into "my corner" of the 12 x 16 stall every day to feed and clean. She stayed well-hidden in her den-like crate until I disappeared. There was not an opportunity to observe her closely or use her as a model. Our task was to keep her as wild as possible, so she would be a good release candidate in the spring. Roger thought that keeping her wild was one of the easiest things he ever did.

It was of course a disappointment to not be able to relate with the bear cub, but the reward came in April 1990 when Houdini was released back into the wild near Chama, New Mexico. She came to us a starving 35 pound cub and was released a wild, fat and healthy 85 pound yearling, ear tag #66. We never inquired as to whether her ear tag was later recovered. We could only wish her a long and healthy life in the mountains where she belonged.

Prairie Picnic, 1990, 15 x 28 x 12 inches

I feel tremendously close to each of my models, yet the subjects are secondary to the concept I am trying to communicate. Katie Heiss modeled for *Prairie Picnic* and *Plucky* modeled as both raccoons.

A composition utilizing strong lines is used to convey a connection between the young woman and the natural world. The sculpture acknowledges people all over the world who are taking stewardship of the land and are caring for animals.

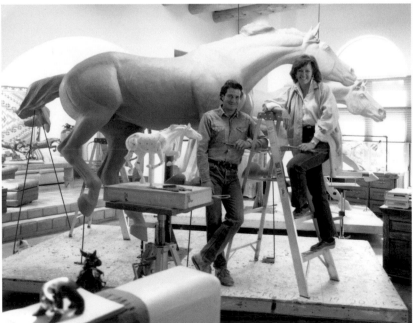

I worked with only one assistant. We kept two horses in progress at a time. As each horse was finished, my assistant Brett Chomer, would mold the horse. After the mold was removed, the clay was stripped from the armature for application to the next horse in line. The completed armature went very unceremoniously to the dump, and the next armature was built. Each horse took approximately six months to sculpt.

The molds were shipped from Santa Fe to Valley Bronze in Joseph, Oregon to be cast in bronze. Each bronze horse weighs about 1,500 pounds, is cast hollow, and is fully engineered with structural stainless steel inside the body and legs. Lely required that each horse had to withstand 110 mph winds. The Freedom Horses were tested shortly after installation when Hurricane Andrew swept through Naples, Florida in 1992. They remained unscathed.

The Freedom Horses

My Santa Fe dream studio included a raised 12' x 12' model stage. The horse stall-sized space was equipped with rubber mats and double exterior doors to facilitate bringing horses directly into the studio. Rails kept the horses from stepping down into my work space.

The call from John Agneli of the Lely Development Corporation was perfectly timed. He invited me to submit a design to create five over life-sized-horses. It was the perfect opportunity to utilize my new studio and do a major sculpture of the subject I knew best and loved most.

I began by creating 6" tall studies of the five horses in an interesting composition. Since the horses were to be free-running, I utilized classic horse behavior and placed the stallion behind the mares.

The next step was to create accurate 1/4 life-sized working models or "maquettes." I work directly from life so the selection of models was important. A hunter/jumper trainer in Santa Fe provided two beautiful thoroughbred mares. They were brought to my barn one at a time to model.

A very special horse named "Rising Star" was boarded next door at Rancho Encantado. Rising Star was the horse that co-starred with Robert Redford in *Electric Horseman*. With Redford's permission, Star became my model for the stallion.

After the working models were completed and approved by Lely, the enlarging process began. The Freedom Horses were sculpted in the centuries old "point up" method. Each working model was fixed to a board that was marked with a 1" square grid. The monumental horses, which were to be enlarged five times, were on rolling pallets marked with a 5" grid. The armature, or support system for each horse, was welded steel sprayed with foam insulation. The foam was carved back to approximate the form of each horse. Even with the foam core, each horse had about 1,200 pounds clay applied to complete the sculpture.

Freedom Stallion

The model for the stallion was "Rising Star" who co-stared with Robert Redford in the movie *The Electric Horseman*. After the movie, Redford bought the horse and later loaned him to me to use in this sculpture.

Freedom Horses, Lely Resort - Naples, Florida, 1992

The Day the Wall Came Down

A MONUMENT TO FREEDOM by Roger Brooks

For 28 years, the Berlin Wall stood as the most visible example of the Iron Curtain defining Soviet-controlled Europe. Berlin was located well within the part of Germany occupied by the Soviet Union as a consequence of World War II. Germany had been divided into East Germany and West Germany with a portion of Berlin, the capitol city, under the control of Western powers and the remainder of the city controlled by the Soviet Union. In 1948, the Soviets attempted to starve West Berlin into alignment with East Germany by cutting off ground access through East Germany. Their plan was thwarted by the Western allies with the creation of the Berlin Airlift, which flew massive amounts of food, fuel and clothing to those stranded in West Berlin, breaking the siege a year and a half later. In 1961 the Soviets acted again by building a 105 mile long and 14 foot tall concrete wall around West Berlin, not to keep its inhabitants in, but to keep East Germans from fleeing Communist East Germany to sanctuary in West Berlin.

When this despicable barrier was breached on November 9, 1989, it was the beginning of the end of Communism in Europe. One year later Germany once again became a single nation and the Soviet Union itself dissolved two years later. To commemorate the victory of free people over the forces of totalitarian rule, artists from all over the world offered pieces of art to celebrate the fall of the Berlin Wall. Berlin refused all these offers except for one, the sculpture *The Day The Wall Came Down*.

Horses have always been used in art a symbol of freedom. By Veryl using horses to represent Germans breaking through a barrier to their own freedom, this sculpture also represents other people seeking to overcome obstacles to their own personal freedom. As someone once said, "This sculpture carries no flag, yet it carries everyone's flag."

The Day the Wall Came Down was unveiled at the Allied Museum in Berlin,
Germany on July 2, 1998.

It is 1 1/4 life-sized, 12 feet high x 30 feet long x 12 feet wide and weighs seven tons.
There are only two monumental castings of *The Day the Wall Came Down* — sister castings.
The American casting was first displayed in Atlanta, Georgia, at Stone Mountain Park during
the 1996 Olympic Games before moving to its permanent home at the George H. W. Bush
Presidential Library at Texas A&M University, August 1997.

Veryl and former ambassador to Germany, Vernon Walters, with the first "working model" casting

November 9, 1989 began as a normal day, but by the time it was over our lives had been changed. News during the day was that the Berlin Wall had opened and East Berliners were streaming into West Berlin. Veryl and I were transfixed as we watched world history in the making.

By coincidence, Veryl was then sculpting five running horses, miniatures in clay. We went to bed that night comfortable with the thought that something unimaginable had just happened. For 28 years the Berlin Wall withstood all efforts to tear it down. That night Veryl had a dream that her little sculpted horses were the ones who were running through the breach in the Berlin Wall to freedom in the West. It was this dream that changed our lives. Veryl rose early the next morning and went directly into her studio. By the time I wandered in to see what she was doing, Veryl had her five little horses flying through clay rubble meant as remnants of the Berlin Wall. This little clay sculpture somehow had a dynamic presence that was much larger than its actual size. We gave the sculpture a name, it was *The Day The Wall Came Down.*

A few days later, Lely called to tell Veryl that she had been selected to create their horse sculptures. The design was for five over life-size horses, a stallion and four mares, running through a water feature. After a day or two we came to a decision. A great piece of art has two components; high-quality execution by the artist is one, and the other is the message the art sends to the viewer. I had full confidence that Veryl could sculpt excellent larger-than-life-horses. It was the second component, what this sculpture means, that made our decision. To have Veryl's sculpted horses running through the rubble of the Berlin Wall would represent not just freedom for East Germans, but become a message to all people seeking their individual freedom. It was this larger meaning that overpowered our common sense. Veryl turned down the commission.

Lely called again, this time asking if Veryl would sculpt their horses and use the same horse molds to help create *The Day The Wall Came*

Down. This was a compromise solution we couldn't refuse. Veryl agreed to sculpt the *Lely Freedom Horses*, and we had the right to pursue *The Day The Wall Came Down*, using the same molds as their horses. Veryl, whose interest in history normally centers on the American West and not the Cold War, was insistent that there should only be two monumental castings, one for America and one for Germany. But how were we going to accomplish the creation of a complicated international art project involving two nations, and to do so from Tesuque, New Mexico? We didn't know.

That question was partially answered when the phone rang. It was a couple who had a few of Veryl's sculptures calling from a car phone. They

The Day The Wall Came Down on display in Denver
This casting now resides at the Allied Museum in
Berlin, Germany

were in Santa Fe and wanted to visit Veryl's studio. Having a car phone in 1990 was a big deal so we were already impressed as we awaited our visitors. While showing them around, Veryl pulled out the little study of *The Day The Wall Came Down* and told them what we were hoping to accomplish. They were taken by the concept and later said "The sculpture carries no flag, yet it carries everyone's flag." They then agreed to fund both monuments and give one to the United States and the other to Germany. Our biggest problem was solved.

The next step was to go to Berlin so Veryl could see, photograph and measure the Berlin Wall. The Berlin Wall was still intact in most places, so we were able to feel the ominous nature of this cruel barrier to political freedom. Veryl took photos and measurements as we walked not just along the wall but in the "death strip" between what was actually two huge parallel concrete walls with a "no man's land" between them. We met East Berliners and heard their stories of life in a repressive Communist society.

Now for the easy part. We would offer a huge and meaningful bronze sculpture to the people of Germany as a gift from the people of America. We made an appointment with a ranking cultural official in Berlin so we could present our gift. The man rather coldly reviewed our presentation, looked at us and simply said, "It is impossible. To have such a sculpture there must be a competition and only German artists can apply." We thought he was being quite short-sighted, but we were now stymied. What we did learn from this experience is that the American mind thinks differently. We do not begin with a conclusion that something is impossible; we define problems and then go about solving them. However, here we were, offering a valuable piece of art as a gift from a nation that was Germany's most important partner in defeating Communism, and all we received in return was "it is impossible."

But our luck was not all bad. We visited Checkpoint Charlie and its wonderful museum dedicated to the inhumanity of the Berlin Wall. There we met the man who created the Checkpoint Charlie Museum as his personal protest against the Berlin Wall, Dr. Rainer Hildebrandt. Dr. Hildebrandt was very supportive of the sculpture, which gave us quite a bit of relief and encouragement. Next we visited a film producer who had the most archival film of the Berlin Wall going up, escapes over the wall, and finally, the absolute joy shared around the world when the Berlin Wall was finally breached. Veryl always felt that we needed a short video explaining the sculpture and the Berlin Wall, so we hoped to be able to afford to buy a minute or two of footage. Ernst Wallenberg looked at Veryl's presentation, thought for a while then said, "Some artists have talent but no ideas. Some artists have ideas but no talent. You have both. I will give you all the footage you need to support your sculpture project." Now we started feeling like our mission was not impossible after all. While encouraged, we still had no idea of how difficult it would be to give Germany a piece of sculpture. But ignorance knows no bounds and off we went. With knowledge gained from our trip to Berlin, Veryl sculpted a one-quarter life-size "working model" of *The Day The Wall Came Down*.

Our benefactor had provided us with enough money to cover our foundry costs to complete the first monument, the one slated for Berlin. Veryl cast this sculpture at Valley Bronze Foundry in the town of Joseph, Oregon. The foundry's manager was Karl Fechner, who was born in Germany, and whose grandmother was forced to spend her life in East Germany. As the sculpture neared completion, our next problem became where could we place this huge sculpture until it left for Germany? Veryl and I met with the mayor of Denver, Wellington Webb. Mayor Webb and his wife Wilma, were taken by this 14,000 pound bronze sculpture. At 30 feet long, 18 feet wide and 12 feet high, the sculpture needed a very large sculpture pad. The Mayor offered Veryl just that, a premium site near

George Bush with Helmut Kohl at the George
H. W. Bush Presidential Library

downtown Denver, on an unused helicopter pad. The sculpture arrived with much fanfare, and its unveiling included a man who would later become vital to us, the former American Army Commandant of Berlin, General John Mitchell.

So we now had one monumental sculpture completed with the foundry costs behind us. But we slid to a halt when our benefactor told us that he was unable to further fund the two monuments or provide the political contacts necessary to place them in the United States and Germany. He wished us luck. Now we really needed some luck, much more of it than we originally thought. We made contact with Colorado's German consel, Hans von Barby. Again, Hans was enthusiastic about the sculpture and made some initial contacts in Germany. General Mitchell became increasingly intrigued to the point where he and Hans formed the Berlin Sculpture Fund to work through the political and financial obstacles of placing the sculpture in Berlin.

Next to enter our lives were Joe Hiram Moore and his wife Betty. The Moore's owned a few of Veryl's sculptures and became interested in *The Day The Wall Came Down*, not for Germany but for the United States. Joe was a huge supporter of Texas A&M University that was offering former president George H. W. Bush land near their campus for his presidential library. Since Mr. Bush was our president when the Berlin Wall fell, the Moore's believed his library should be the location for the American casting. Through the Moore's, we were able to meet with President Bush who personally approved the sculpture to be part of his library. The Moore's had assistance from Atlanta resident Jerry Eickhoff and then Georgia's U.S. Senator Paul Coverdell in bringing about the decision by president Bush to accept Veryl's sculpture.

The George H. W. Bush Presidential Library was slated to open in 1997. Jerry Eickhoff and Senator Coverdell had an idea that if the American casting were completed a year early, it could be on display in Atlanta for the 1996 Olympic Games. Stone Mountain State Park, near Atlanta was to be a venue for several events, and Stone Mountain's director Curtis Branscomb was favorable to displaying the sculpture. The Moore's provided the initial funding to begin casting the American sculpture and initiated a fundraising effort towards its permanent placement at the Bush Presidential Library. The sculpture arrived at Stone Mountain in plenty of time for the Olympics, and it was given a premier sculpture site for the next year. We moved the sculpture to the Bush Presidential Library in College Station, Texas in August 1997, just before the library opened to the public. So far, so good.

President Bush, Veryl and Berlin Mayor Diepgen at the sculpture dedication

We were still making only minor progress in placing the German casting in Berlin. A few years earlier, almost by chance, we had dinner in Santa Fe with then Congressman Bill Richardson. During dinner, Veryl told Congressman Richardson about *The Day The Wall Came Down*. General Mitchell and the Berlin Sculpture Fund were having a frustrating time trying to get through Berlin's political bureaucracy. I took a chance and wrote now United Nations Ambassador, Bill Richardson, about the problems we were encountering. Ambassador Richardson contacted the German U.N. ambassador, asking for assistance. The bureaucratic delays soon ended. Another bit of luck was German Chancellor Helmut Kohl had previously seen the sculpture while in Denver attending an economic summit. He and his ambassador to the United States walked and, as I heard, even crawled all through the sculpture while reading the "graffiti" Veryl had painted on the west side of the bronze Berlin Wall. Chancellor Kohl gave his endorsement of *The Day The Wall Came Down*, which added considerable importance to the sculpture project.

The Checkpoint Charlie Stiftung, a Berlin based non-profit, provided invaluable assistance as we bounced our way through Berlin's many twists

USAF flight crew with four of the sculpted
horses at Tempelhof Airport

and turns. We were now long past the "it is impossible" phase. We now
knew it was going to happen, we just didn't know when. After the Berlin
Wall became history, Berlin received more than 1,000 offers from artists
to commemorate the event. Berlin rejected all the artistic statements except
for one, *The Day The Wall Came Down*. During our trips to Berlin, we
now stayed in a nice hotel and, thanks to Berlin's Mayor Diepgen, we had
a black Mercedes with a driver at our disposal. We were given the choice
of several sculpture sites to choose from, including Berlin's famous Tier-
garten. Veryl made the choice and it was a wise one. She chose the new
Allied Museum in the former American-occupied sector of West Berlin.
Veryl felt that over time, the 28-year history of the Berlin Wall and the
sculpture's relevance to this piece of world history would fade. A museum
setting was necessary so that in future years, the story could continue to
be told.

Now our main problem became transporting the sculpture to Berlin.
The Berlin Sculpture Fund had limited success in finding donors for the
sculpture project and had no money to transport the sculpture. Also none
to compensate Veryl for her several years of effort to create this huge
work of art. Again by chance, I had previously met the Air Force Chief
of Staff, General Ron Fogleman in Washington at a reception. General
Fogleman noted at the time that I was from Santa Fe and mentioned that
he had property near Durango, Colorado, a half-day's drive away. Now
that transportation was the current problem, based upon my 30 second
conversation, I wrote General Fogleman to suggest that Veryl's sculpture
could become part of the Berlin Airlift's 50th anniversary celebration in
June 1998. That is only if the Air Force would simply fly the sculpture to

Berlin for us. General Fogleman responded that delivery of the sculpture would provide great symbolism for the sacrifices our airmen made in keeping Berlin from starving during the 1947-1948 Soviet blockade of West Berlin. Yes, the Air Force would fly the sculpture to Berlin, but only as part of a normal supply flight to Germany. We had this problem solved.

Again, good fortune entered during a 1997 summer rodeo Veryl and I attended in Wyoming. The rodeo was held on the ranch of Erivan and Helga Haub. One of their guests was former U.S. Senator Allen Simpson and his wife Ann. The Simpson's collected some of Veryl's sculpture and had known Veryl for about 20 years. During the rodeo I was sitting next to Senator Simpson, so I told him about Veryl's sculpture going to Berlin and that the U.S. Air Force would fly it there. Senator Simpson said that if I had any trouble, let him know as he was a good friends of the Secretary of Defense. I thanked him and told the senator that the transportation issue was "in the bag," but in case we had problems, he would become my "secret agent."

We then made contact with the senior President Bush's office in Houston, informing them of the impending dedication and inviting Mr. Bush to unveil the sculpture. I informed his office that the sculpture would be delivered to Berlin on June 26, 1998 by the U.S. Air Force. President Bush accepted the invitation and said he would plan to be there to unveil it. After so many years this was finally coming together. A month or two later, Veryl and I were watching the news on TV, and there was General Fogleman on the screen, announcing his early retirement from the Air Force. The plans changed because the new Chief of Staff was not intending to place a private piece of art on an Air Force airplane, regardless of the importance of the art or the symbolic gesture to Germany. All the obstacles in Berlin had been eliminated. Our president at the time the Berlin Wall fell, whose diplomacy turned this tactical victory, into a strategic victory would be there, but would Veryl's sculpture? It was now too late to ship this very large sculpture by sea. So, I did the only thing I could think of. I contacted our secret agent, Senator Simpson. Senator Simpson contacted the Secretary of Defense, who contacted the Air Force Chief of Staff. The general agreed that because of the previous commitment, the Air Force would fly the sculpture to Berlin, as long as the State Department paid for the flight. The State Department refused to allocate any of their limited budget to solve a problem for the Air Force, so once again the issue was presented to the Secretary of Defense. As a result the Air Force was instructed to fly the sculpture and to do so on its own budget. Another

C-17 "The Spirit of Berlin" unloading Veryl's sculpture at Berlin's Tempelhof Airport on June 26, 1998.

Pictured are the airplane crew on the left and members of the German Army on the right

The Central Intelligence Agency presented Veryl with the Agency Seal Medallion, shown above, on October 5, 2000.

problem solved and the way was again clear. That is until President Bush's office called me. President Bush would be in Paris just prior to the unveiling in Berlin, and would I please provide him and his seven Secret Service agents with a business jet to take them from Paris to Berlin and, of course, return. I saw our efforts coming down around our ears if I couldn't find a way to get President Bush, who Germans referred to as being "the father of German reunification," to Berlin to unveil Veryl's sculpture. But we couldn't afford the many thousands of dollars it would take to charter an eight passenger business jet. We were saved when our Air Force command in Europe thought it best if they were the ones who flew our former president to Berlin. We agreed with their decision.

Denver gave the sculpture a grand farewell. Mayor Webb presided, along with Denver's mounted police, a Colorado National Guard F-16 flyover, speeches, bands and lots of American flags. Children tied candy to the sculpture for German children to have, symbolizing the candy our military "candy bombers" dropped to West Berlin's children during the Berlin Airlift. The sculpture was first moved by truck to Charleston AFB where it was loaded on a giant C-17 cargo plane. Veryl and I flew commercially to Germany, meeting up with the sculpture at Ramstein AFB in Germany. The symbolism of our Air Force delivering this sculpture to Berlin's Tempelhof Airport on the 50th anniversary of the first Berlin Airlift flight was further enhanced by the specific plane chosen for the mission. This almost brand new plane had a special meaning bestowed upon it by President Clinton and Germany's Chancellor Kohl. A few months earlier they had christened the plane *The Spirit of Berlin.* On the flight from Ramstein north to Berlin, Veryl and I had the honor of being seated in cockpit jump seats. When we descended over Berlin with the sculpture, our proud and enthused pilots requested a low level lap or two around the city which was followed by their historic 50th anniversary landing. The airplane was met by a contingent of people important to the project. The German Army transported the sculpture to its permanent residence, the brand new Allied Museum in a traffic stopping military convoy.

The German Army with their manpower and cranes helped Karl Fechner and myself with the installation. On July 2, 1998, Veryl, President George H. W. Bush, General John Mitchell and Berlin's mayor Eberhard Diepgen unveiled *The Day The Wall Came Down* in front of distinguished guests, a gaggle of press and, of course, seven Secret Service agents.

In this book's preface, Veryl makes mention that it took "a village" to help her develop her talents. This project, creating and delivering Veryl's 14,000 pound bronze monument to freedom to the once captive city of West Berlin took a village by itself. Our journey was nine years start to finish, and it literally changed our lives.

We will always remember Berlin, that little island of freedom in the heart of Communist Europe. *The Day The Wall Came Down* sculpture stands in honor of Berlin, the city that made the fatal tear in the fabric of the Iron Curtain.

July 4th celebration, George H. W. Bush Presidential Library.

"Other than the perception of the planting of our flag on Mount Suribachi on Iwo Jima during World War II, there is no other image which portrays the concept of freedom, liberty, and the American spirit than a herd of horses running free. This image has been used numerously by artists exemplifying the freedom of America." John Geraghty

No Turning Back

No Turning Back — working model,
1993, 18 x 14 x 9 inches

I came out of the antique store rolling a wagon wheel. Roger helped me load it into the car with the obvious question. I didn't know just yet, but before we got back to Santa Fe, *No Turning Back* had taken shape in my mind.

Starting in the early 1840's, the westward expansion of the United States became a flood of ox-drawn covered wagons. Lands were opened for homesteaders willing to risk the dangers of crossing the plains and the Rocky Mountains to find prosperity in the fertile soil out west. Women were very much a part of these caravans. Some were married and had children. Some gave birth along the trail. Others were widowed or were independent entrepreneurs who chose to never marry. The only certainty on the trail west was once you began, there was "no turning back."

No Turning Back is without a doubt one of my most significant works. It seems to be timeless in that it has been reproduced on the cover of a CD album in which a song was composed from the accompanying poem I wrote. Arizona Highways used an image of the sculpture on the cover of a book titled *Stalwart Women.* Every major western art magazine has used an image of *No Turning Back,* and it was featured in *Sculptors of the Rockies,* a book produced by *Southwest Art* magazine in 2009.

I had a calico dress made that was an exact replica of the dresses that were commonly worn during the 1860's on the westbound wagon trails. A young woman, Jessica La Casse, was recommended as an ideal model. I connected with Jessica the second I met her. She was perfect with large eyes, long wavy hair and a physical grace that never failed to inspire me. She was only 16. Jessica and I discussed how the young women heading west into the unknown had to be filled with trepidation. She leaned onto the wagon wheel, looked back down the imaginary trail and brought her

No Turning Back, 1993,
66 inches high

hand to her throat in a perfect gesture of apprehension. The composition simply fell into place with that gesture.

No Turning Back graces the entrance to the home of John and Saralynne Geraghty, in California. The Geraghty's have one of the most significant collections of western art in the world. The sculpture is also at the Old West Museum in Cheyenne, Wyoming and in the center of St. Joseph, Missouri. Art patron, John Koontz, gave a life-sized casting to YMCA Camp Tecumseh in Brookston, Indiana to encourage young women and teach them history. The image of *No Turning Back* on the cover of this book was taken at the private residence of David and Sandi Whitmore in Libertyville, Illinois.

No Turning Back — working model,
1993, 18 x 14 x 9 inches

NO TURNING BACK

Too young and naive
to think they could fail
Too full of visions
for the end of the trail
They stored their silk dresses
and donned calico
To join in the cry
of Westward Ho

Their diaries tell
of the endless hours
The vast sea of grass
and bounty of wildflowers
They tell of children
conceived and born
And of those who were buried
in the gray silent morn

Still the wagons rolled on
and the ruts got deeper
The column moved westward
as the route got steeper
Teams dropped from exhaustion
in the summer heat
As the emigrants pressed on
defying defeat

They met Indians who were friends
and many that were foe
They saw days of drought
and blinding snow
Only one thing was certain
along this wagon track

There was absolutely
No Turning Back

by Veryl Goodnight

107

Veryl's Girls by Barbara van Cleve
Models left to right: Gloria Begay, Kari Taylor,
Kathleen Owegone, Veryl, Jessica LaCasse

The animal and human relationship is a common theme in my work. Often times the animals are working partners with the figures but sometimes they are a metaphor for something other than themselves.

Such is the case in *Looks Are Deceiving*. Kari Taylor was a beautiful and independent young woman working at Zaplin-Lambert Gallery on Canyon Road in Santa Fe. Unlike the uncertain woman in *No Turning Back*, this woman had control of all that surrounded her.

The split skirt that became popular in the 1910's was a major step toward independence as women began to ride horses "astride."

LOOKS ARE DECEIVING

It is well-known

  That a Cat is self-possessed

    Choosing to lie alone

      Then demanding to be caressed.

It is the Cat's allure

  To be deceiving

    To make you unsure

      Of the message you are receiving.

One look should explain

  From beneath the wide-brimmed hat

    That their souls are the same

      The Cowgirl and the Cat.

by Veryl Goodnight

Looks Are Deceiving, 1994, 24 x 12 x 9 inches

Shepherds of the Nation, 1994, 15 x 14 x 14 inches

Other Cultures

Artists' surroundings have a tremendous influence on their work and their choice of subject matter. The wildlife was sparse around Santa Fe. I saw coyotes and ravens, but there really wasn't much else to be seen in the pinyon-juniper country.

History, on the other hand, was everywhere. I am a prolific reader, and I became fascinated with the difference in cultures. I originally intended to portray women from several cultures. My first venture took me into Navajo country. I had collected Navajo rugs for many years and needed one repaired. Mary Lea Begay was recommend to make the repair. Roger and I met Mary Lea Begay in Grants, New Mexico. She came with her mother and daughter, Gloria, who translated for her. Gloria was beautiful and very shy when I asked her is she would consider modeling for me.

I spent three wonderful days with Gloria and her family near Ganado doing research for the sculpture. She came out dressed in fine velvet and wearing family jewelry. I took dozens of photos of Gloria with sheep on their ranch. We then spent a day in Monument Valley where Gloria again wore family jewelry and good clothes. It didn't feel right. When Gloria asked me what was wrong, I replied, "What would your grandmother have worn when herding sheep?"

The next day she happily jumped in my car when I went to pick her up for our day in Canyon de Chelly. She was wearing a cotton broom skirt, working moccasins; her old shirt was closed with a single turquoise pin and her hair hung loose. She smiled and said "I didn't even put cream on my legs." That is the day I got the reference that resulted in *Shepherds of the Nation*. The sculpture itself was completed during the summer of 1994 when Gloria came to live with us for several months. I used my own border collie, Robin, as the model for the dog.

The Gathering, 1995, 26 x 16 x 10 inches

The grocery store of the pioneer women was in their backyard — the garden, chickens and milk cows. Animals were often more than a source for food, however. Evetts Haley wrote about Charlie Goodnight's wife, Mary Ann. She was the only white woman for miles in the newly settled Palo Duro Canyon. The cowboys brought her three chickens, which she turned into pets.

I "rented" three chickens as models for *The Gathering*. They lived on my studio stage in a bed of straw for several weeks, providing fresh eggs along with inspiration.

Reflections, 1996, 19 x 17 x 10 inches

Reflections was a commission to commemorate the 50th anniversary of the Round Up Riders, a group of men based in Denver, who do a week long ride each year. The idea for *Reflections* came while riding Gwalowa on the ridges above our home. We would stop at the top of steep trails so I could dismount before descending into the arroyos. We'd pause together and look out across the valley. The gesture of a rider and his horse looking into the distance seemed to speak to fifty years of dedication and camaraderie the Round Up Riders had with their own horses.

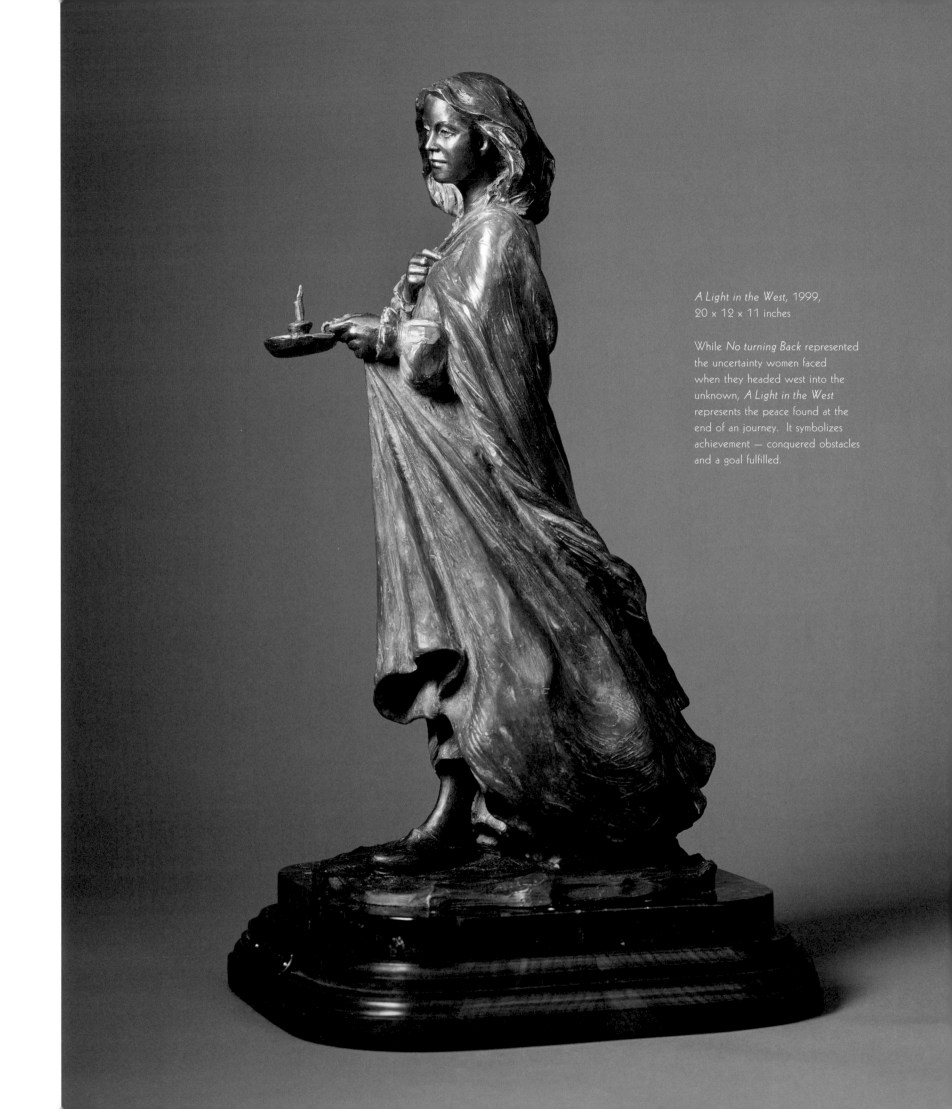

A Light in the West, 1999,
20 × 12 × 11 inches

While *No turning Back* represented
the uncertainty women faced
when they headed west into the
unknown, *A Light in the West*
represents the peace found at the
end of an journey. It symbolizes
achievement — conquered obstacles
and a goal fulfilled.

Second Thoughts, 1999, 6 feet 3 inches x
6 feet 6 inches x 30 inches

Matt Dillon is half Arabian and half Quarter Horse. I purchased him largely due to his near perfect conformation and generic good looks. He modeled for five different sculptures, but *Second Thoughts* remains my personal favorite.

I was interested in creating a quiet scene. Cats are curious but are notorious cowards. Dillon reached down to greet Tina and she immediately had second thoughts. Dillon and Tina moved with us from New Mexico to Colorado. Both are now retired and still share the same barn.

Creating Larger Works
USING DIGITAL TECHNOLOGY

Digital photography and digital enlarging are great assets today. I shoot digital video at 23 frames a second and then download only a few seconds of action so I can study the movement of my subject. The rise and fall of a horse's mane or the flare of the nostril can now be observed in synch with a given footfall. Ultimately this makes both sculpture and painting more convincing.

Digital enlargement of a working model not only saves me hundreds of hours of tedious enlarging and hundreds of pounds of expensive clay; it allows me to re-interpret my own maquette at a larger scale. Assistants were mandatory when using the ancient method of enlarging with a plumb bob and grid. Often their interpretations of my work would take more effort to correct than if I had sculpted it in the first place. For instance an average horse's neck is only 9" thick. I spent hours removing pounds of clay from a neck my assistant had enlarged to 24 inches thick in spite of my accurate working model. He just did not believe that a horse's neck was that slender.

It is important to stay excited about a large sculpture during the many months of sculpting. The older enlargement methods felt more like a construction job, and I got horribly bored and anxious to begin a new idea. The high cost of a digitally enlarged foam armature is a minor consideration compared to staying excited about a sculpture through completion.

While highly detailed enlarging is available, I prefer a less detailed enlargement in dense blue foam. This foam can be cut easily without creating the fine powder of the harder yellow foam. I sculpt much more "information" in the larger sculpture, so all I really desire from the foam enlargement is a sophisticated and structurally sound armature that replicates the original movement and proportions. I also strive for a final surface that has the vibrancy and texture of thicker clay.

Scent of Spring, 1993, 10 x 11 x 5 inches

Sprite, 1999, 5 feet 6 inches x 5 feet 6 inches x 24 inches

Second Thoughts was the last enlargement I sculpted using the plumb bob and grid method. *Sprite* was the first enlargement using a digitally enlarged foam armature.

117

Thinning the Forest, 19xx, 24 x 36 inches

Sunrise on the Gold Rush Trail, 2000, 16 x 20 inches

During the spring of 1999, I joined a small wagon train for a few days as they traveled across Southern Colorado to California commemorating the 150th anniversary of the Gold Rush. I took my own horse, Toddy, and slept in the Conestoga wagons at night.

PASSING TIMES

A promise of prosperity
    beckoned from the west
Seducing men and women
    to the ultimate test

Homes were left behind
    and possessions trimmed to few
Still the women took their manners
    as they headed West to begin anew

How could they know
    that on the wild and open range
Their proper saddles and flowing skirts
    would be against the winds of change

Modesty would soon give way
    to the demands of the rugged land
And fashion took second place
    to being a good hand

The younger girls
    were quickest to learn
That riding astride in a skirt divided
    provided the freedom for which they yearned

We still live today in Passing Times
    whether in the home or on the range
We have a choice of riding
    with or against the winds of change

by Veryl Goodnight

Details from the original version of *Passing Times*, 1993, 36 x 50 x 30 inches

Passing Times was initially inspired through a gift from a lady who presented me with her grandmother's western sidesaddle. The saddle, made by the S. C. Gallup Saddlery Company in Pueblo, Colorado, is an exact replica of the one that Charles Goodnight designed for Mary Ann.

The western frontier became a stage for women to break loose from antiquated laws and customs of the East. Sidesaddles and long skirts were, in a practical sense, dangerous.

I chose models that were a generation apart in age to illustrate the transition. I wanted the older woman to be curious, rather than judgmental when observing the younger rider. As is so often the case, when I explained this goal to my model, Kathleen Owegone simply tipped her head and the gesture said everything. She is riding into the wind with her proper attire and sidesaddle. Kari Taylor was equally adept in portraying nonchalant freedom as the younger astride rider. She is a picture of practicality as she rides with the winds of change.

The original 35" high version of *Passing Times* is in six museums or public collections and a bas-relief silhouette of the sculpture is included in the frieze along the top of The Cowgirl Hall of Fame building in Forth Worth, Texas. The 18" high version was created by popular demand to accommodate private collectors.

Passing Times, 2000, 18 x 22 x 15 inches

Mending the Flag, 2002, 17 x 16 x 13 inches

September 11, 2001 is one of the dates in history that we all remember where we were. I was in Jackson, Wyoming, in a log cabin on Wilson Creek. My own reality seemed so twisted as I looked out at a bull moose crossing the creek with only a few yards separating him from the horror we were watching on the television screen.

A week later as we drove home to Santa Fe through Wyoming, Colorado, and half of New Mexico, I was uplifted by the American flags displayed absolutely everywhere. I began searching for a meaningful way to portray the show of solidarity we were witnessing. A few months later I saw a brilliant little painting by my friend Buck McCain of an American Flag stretched out over a table as a woman mended it. With Buck's blessing, I reworked his concept into a sculptural composition. Thus, *Mending the Flag* was born.

Back From the Brink

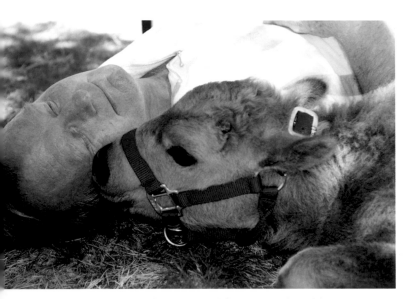

Charlie with his new "mom" Roger at 10 days old

By 1878 the millions of buffalo that once blackened the prairies of West Texas were a thing of the past. For two years since settling their ranch in the Palo Duro Canyon, Colonel Charles Goodnight and his wife, Mary Ann, had heard the reports of the Sharps rifles day and night. The hide hunters were mercilessly slaughtering every bison they could find.

It was Mary Ann who revolted and persuaded her husband to protect the small number of bison that had sought refuge in a remote corner of the Palo Duro. Goodnight's cowboys roped two calves and brought them to Mary Ann to care for. These two calves and others that were captured later became the nucleus of the herd that saved the Southern bison herd from complete extinction. Stock from the Goodnight herd was vital in bringing both the Northern and Southern bison herds back from the brink of extinction. Progeny from the Goodnight herd were distributed across the United States to help rebuild other herds including the one in Yellowstone National Park.

To create *Back From The Brink*, I sent out several letters to bison ranches asking for the opportunity to raise an orphan calf should one become available. Marlo Goble of Medicine Lodge Buffalo Ranch near Dubois, Idaho called in May, 2000. The post lady had noticed a newborn calf all alone while on her rural ranch route. Little "Charlie" had become separated from his mother when the herd had been moved the day before and survived his first night of life alone. Roger flew us to Idaho immediately, and we brought Charlie home to Santa Fe in our plane. We bottle-raised Charlie with the intent of returning him to Idaho when the sculpture was finished. However, Charlie had other plans.

Charlie became inseparably bonded to Roger, his new mom. Roger fell under the spell of this little bull calf who would lie under his office window in order to stay as close to him as possible. Roger had all kinds of excuses for not taking Charlie back to Idaho, and Marlo eventually gave Charlie to Roger as a gift.

Back From The Brink, 2000, 24 x 19 x 17 inches

Since Charlie was imprinted as a result of being bottle-raised, we attempted to do the right thing and teach him how to be a buffalo. After he was weaned in January, we took him to the Montosa Buffalo Ranch near Taos, and he was put in with two other weanling bison calves. Sometime during the night, however, Charlie must have become frightened, for he ran head on into a steel fence. He was paralyzed. Roger and I took turns sitting up with him throughout the day and the bitter cold nights of January 3 and 4, 2001. When it became apparent that he wasn't going to be able to stand on his own, four men lifted him into our horse trailer. We took him to Colorado State University's veterinary hospital where he was diagnosed with severe spinal cord trauma.

Charlie spent almost four weeks in a sling attached to a hoist so he could be raised and lowered and he learned to walk again by being pushed along a track. As soon as Charlie was able to get up and down on his own, we brought him back to Santa Fe to recuperate. Roger was tireless in his care for this now 550 pound ten month old buffalo calf. They made quite a sight hiking together up the arroyos near our home. Roger did everything he could to help Charlie regain full use of his hind legs, which would buckle and cause him to fall. Charlie would never be able to live in a pasture with other buffalo.

Prairie Contender, 2003, 12 x 17 x 8 inches
(Charlie as a 2 year old bull)

Charlie Modeling in Veryl's studio

Back From the Brink (detail life-size), 2001,
6 feet 5 inches x 4 feet 10 inches x 4 feet 8
inches. Shown here at the entrance to the ranch
Erivan and Helga Haub, Cora, Wyoming

Our Gentle Giant

Charlie reached 2,000 pounds and the age of three under Roger's constant care. His weakened neck eventually caused his death. Charlie lay down in the arena on a hot day in the summer of 2003 and was unable to rise. When a bovine is down for an extended period of time, their lungs fill will fluid. After a several-week-long battle, Charlie died in our arms from pneumonia on August 10, 2003.

Charlie's death was a tremendous tragedy in our lives. Roger's devotion to one buffalo was astounding. Charlie lives on in bronze, telling the story of the Goodnights' love of bison from a century earlier. However, it was Richard Rosen, a writer from New York who brought the story of Roger's devotion to the public in a book titled *A Buffalo In the House*.

Charlie studied his image as a one-month-old calf before *Back From The Brink* was taken to The Wildlife Experience in Parker, Colorado. One of the inaugural exhibits of The Wildlife Experience Museum, founded by David and Gail Lininger, was titled *Back From The Brink*. The exhibit featured the sculpture and a short documentary of Charles and Mary Ann Goodnight's role in saving bison from extinction.

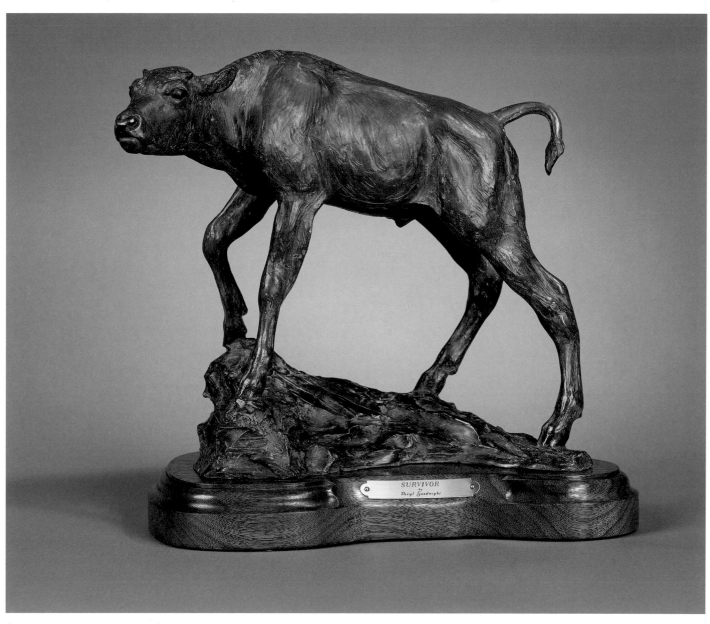

Survivor, 2000, 12 x 14 x 7 inches

Back From The Brink (life-size), 2000, 6 feet 5 inches x 4 feet 10 inches x
4 feet 8 inches. Shown here at Camp Tecumseh, Brookston, Indiana

A Long Stretch, 1999, 11 x 12 x 8 inches

Happy Go Lucky, 2004, 4 feet x 4 feet x 1 foot 6 inches

Golden, 1997, 9 x 14 x 4 inches

My own cats, dogs, and horses are always an inspiration, as are the pets of friends and neighbors. The devotion of Luke, the German Shepherd, helped inspire *Trusty by My Side*. The balance of the inspiration came from reading an account of a woman who defended her home and children from invading Indians with the aid of a dog named Trusty and the rifle over the fireplace. Cathy Smith provided the Colt pump action rifle and historically accurate clothes. Cathy has been the costumer for major films such as *Dances With Wolves*. We first met in Montana during a Northwest Rendezvous Paint Out. Our paths seem to cross no matter where I live and Cathy often assists to insure the authenticity of historic outfits for my models. Celeste Gose, a Wyoming ranch girl, brought an abundance of "don't mess with me" attitude to the sculpture

Trusty by My Side, 1998, 20 x 12 x 10 1/2 inches

Bears can be many things to many people, but all bears can make us laugh — and humor is what I sought when sculpting *Toe Jam*. Tom Saubert arranged for the Northwest Rendezvous artists to spend a day at Animals of Montana near Bozeman, during the 2005 Paint Out. Six month old "Yosemite" played very hard for an hour while all of us filmed, photographed and sketched. Energy spent, he finally plopped down a few feet in front of me and began cleaning his paws.

Toe Jam (Grizzly Bear Cub), 2006, 9 x 12 x 8 inches

The Bronc

The Bronc, 2002, 9 x 7 x 5 inches

The Bronc was one of my most enjoyable and rewarding sculptures. It was enjoyable in that I was able to reconnect with wild horses and their Spanish roots. The model, Tarkio, is registered with The Spanish Mustang Registry, an organization that has helped preserve the original bloodlines from the horses of the Conquest.

This sculpture was a commission for the University of Texas, Pan American campus, in Edinburg, Texas. The student body of this branch of UT was 85% Hispanic and many of the students were the first in their families to receive a higher education. I was commissioned to recreate the school's logo of a bronc with its head down. I chose the Spanish Mustang horse to recognize the heritage of the student body and acknowledge one of the greatest gifts that the Spanish Conquistadors brought to the new world.

Tarkio was well trained – too well trained to actually buck. I digitized a video of rodeo horses in order to play back the motion one frame at a time and select the optimum position that closely resembled the school's logo. I worked directly from Tarkio afterward, utilizing his classic mustang proportions, slight roman nose, and heavy mane and tail.

The unveiling of the over-life-sized bronc was very rewarding. The student body and faculty were so proud to have the sculpture on campus. The school band was composed of mariachis, and the speakers were all of Hispanic origin and gave passionate talks about the opportunities they found in the United States through a higher education at the University of Texas.

The Bronc was also selected for the entrance to The Wildlife Experience Museum in Parker, Colorado. I was very happy to see a museum devoted to wildlife recognize the wild horse as an integral part of American wildlife.

The Bronc, 2002, 11 x 8 x 3 feet
The Wildlife Experience Museum, Parker, Colorado

American Warrior

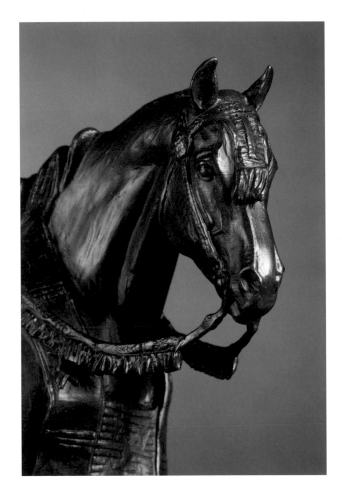

Senator Campbell modeling

American Warrior represents a contemporary Northern Cheyenne chief, Ben Nighthorse Campbell. A genuine hero to the Native Americans, Ben Campbell earned the 72 feathers in his war bonnet as the Captain of the United States Olympic Judo team in the 1964 Olympic Games. Ben went on to excel in everything he has done. He was a winning breeder and trainer of Quarter horses, is an outstanding jeweler, and he served Colorado, as a United States Senator from 1993 to 2005.

When the Smithsonian's National Museum of the American Indian opened in 2004, Ben was invited to show his jewelry in the inaugural exhibit. Ben's wife Linda, and daughter, Shanan Campbell Wells, asked if I would create a sculpture of Ben on his favorite horse to accompany the exhibit.

Our friendship began in the 1980's as artists in a joint exhibit of his jewelry and my sculpture. I was thrilled to be able to sculpt my friend and simultaneously give him a portrait of the horse he had loved so much. Ben's classic Indian profile and the proud way he sat on "Scamp" as Grand Marshall during the Rose Bowl Parade inspired the composition for *American Warrior.*

American Warrior, 2004, 31 x 28 x 15 inches

American Warrior was exhibited at the Smithsonian's National Museum of the American Indian in 2004
in conjunction with the inaugural exhibit of Senator Ben Nighthorse Campbell's jewelry designs.

Pathfinders, 2001, 19 x 26 x 17 inches

The Wolf Pack

Wolves are one of the most difficult subjects I have undertaken. There are such subtle differences that make the wolf and the dog different from each other. I was fortunate to be able to hike with three high content (98%) wolf dogs to gather the feeling of movement and interaction. My research also took me to The Lamar Valley of Yellowstone National Park. Dr. James Halfpenny taught a course on wolves through the Yellowstone Institute. Winter wolf watching in Lamar Valley is very fruitful.

The details, however, came from full-blooded wolves at a refuge four hours from my home near the Zuni Pueblo. Out of seventy animals, I chose to work from only one - because Genghis was unmistakably A WOLF.

Wolf Pack (details), 2005
Lincoln Park Zoo in Chicago, Illinois

143

Pond's Edge, 2005, 3 feet 3 inches x 7 feet x 2 feet 6 inches

Summer Moon, 2005, 5 feet x 7 feet x 1 foot 5 inches

Night Traveler, 2005, 3 feet 6 inches x 7 feet x 1 foot 8 inches

The Lincoln Park Zoo in Chicago, Illinois commissioned me to enlarge the three wolves from *Pathfinders* to 15% over life-size. These large wolves were installed in 2006 to stand guard over the entrance to the Pritzker Children's Zoo. Two additional sets of the Wolf Pack guard the entrances to The Wildlife Experience Museum south of Denver, Colorado and the Leanin' Tree Sculpture Garden in Boulder, Colorado.

The Wolf Pack was the last sculpture completed during our 18 years in Santa Fe.

Summer Moon (working model), 2004, 17 x 21 x 6 inches

Pond's Edge (working model), 2005, 12 x 21 x 9 inches

Rainy Day, 2006, 24 x 30 inches

Chico at Rest, 2000, 18 x 24 inches

Wild Burros of Piute Mesa, 2002, 24 x 30 inches

PART THREE

Home Again

A Dream Come True

Childhood memories leave deep impressions. Family trips into the Colorado Mountains left me with a life-long desire to live in the high country. In October 2006 that dream was finally realized when Roger and I moved from Santa Fe to Mancos, Colorado.

Roger and I had purchased 57 ponderosa-covered acres in 2005 on the shoulder of the La Plata Mountains. The gently sloping land overlooks irrigated ranches and Mesa Verde National Park to the west. The view to the east is dominated by 12,000 foot high Helmet Peak.

The Middle Mancos River runs through our land. We had a thriving colony of beaver for several years that left us with 14 dams. There is a wildlife corridor between the house and river. We have seen coyotes, deer, a bobcat, a raccoon, skunks, bears and mountain lion tracks on this corridor. During the winter, the wild turkeys take shelter on our patio.

The barn was completed first and includes a large room on the north to serve as a monument studio. When our home sold in Santa Fe, we set up housekeeping in the barn studio while our new home was under construction. Roger and I lived and worked in the barn for two years and two months before moving into our home in time for Thanksgiving 2008.

Roger has a nice office in the house, and I have a secondary studio where I can do small sculptures or paintings. The spaces were very well designed by good friend and talented architect, Melanie Brown. The house fits our needs perfectly.

The barn studio now serves its intended use as a monument studio, a place to teach, and a place to work from live models. There is a "model run" to the west and an overhead garage door that opens into the barn aisle. This allows me to push sculptures out into the sun to study the effects of light on the form. The converted loft serves as a guest room for the heartiest of our friends.

Cani-crossing in red rock country west of Mancos

Helmet Peak from the east windows of Veryl and Rogers' home

151

Away From the Crowd, 2007, 12 x 12 inches

Exhibited at *The Masters of the American West* 2008
Autry National Center, Los Angeles, California

Winter Quarters, 2009, 18 x 24 inches

We are now surrounded by wildlife. As spring fades into summer, mountain meadows are dotted with wildflowers and young animals.

The Mules Ear wildflowers fascinated me as much as the babies themselves. When living so close to the land, the rhythm of the seasons is more apparent.

The land and the animals are one.

High Country Summer in Progress by Lou Swenson

High Country Summer (Life-size), 2009, 44 x 38 x 12 inches

Emergence, 2008, 17 x 29 x 8 inches

A mule deer doe raised twin fawns right outside my studio during our first summer back in Colorado. I was able to observe them until late in the fall. The complex form of the oak brush, from which the deer would emerge into the meadows, created the greatest challenge. As with *High Country Summer*, however, the landscape was inseparable from the deer.

First Winter (detail), 2010, 12 x 16 inches

Blue Bell Cow and Girl

Blue Bell Creamery of Brenham, Texas commissioned me to bring their logo to life to celebrate their 100th anniversary in 2007. Their silhouette of a little girl leading a Jersey cow is well known and proved very "sculptural."

I researched Jersey cattle at Mountain Shadows Dairy in Litchfield, Park, Arizona. The owner was gracious in educating me about Jersey conformation. An ideal cow was selected, videoed, photographed and measured. I sculpted directly from her on several occasions. The little country girl was sculpted from Chessie Kimble in Cortez, Colorado. Video again enabled me to study the movement of both Chessie and the Jersey cow, bringing the silhouette to life from 360 degrees.

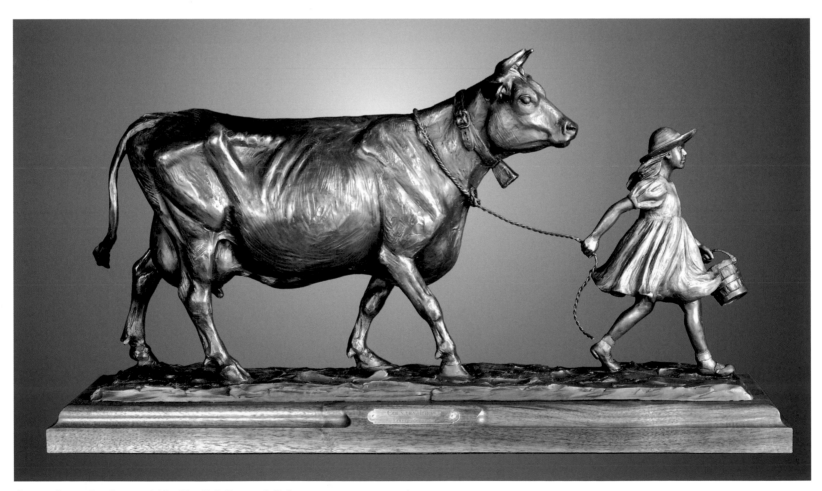

Country Living (working model for Blue Bell Cow and Girl), 2006, 14 x 27 x 5 inches

Blue Bell Cow and Girl, Life-size, 2007, 61 x 120 x 28 inches
Blue Bell Creamery, Brenham, Texas

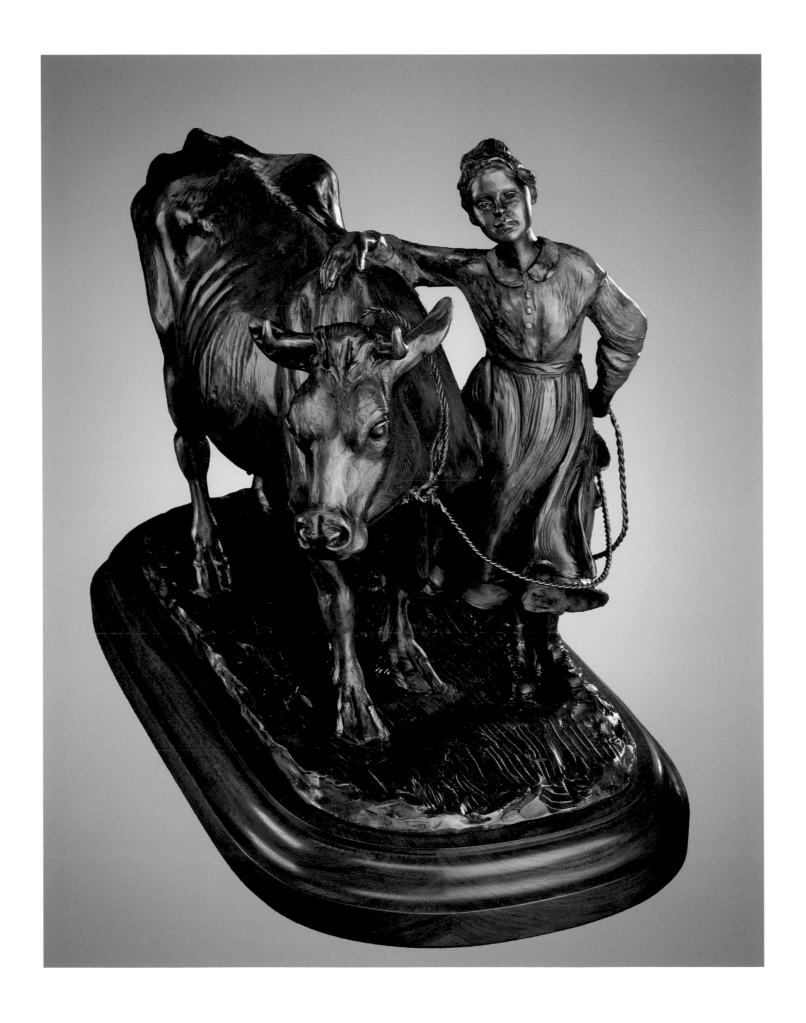

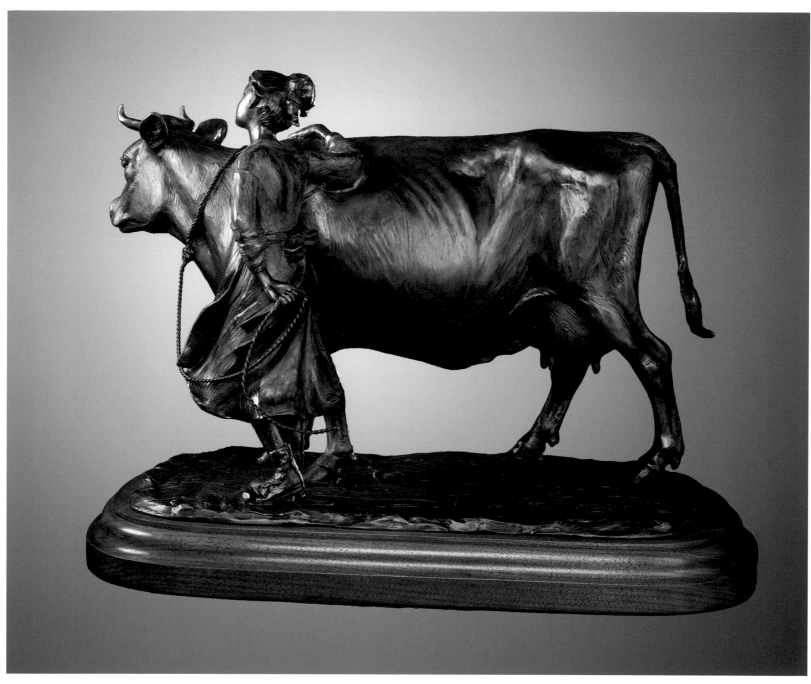

Daydreaming, 2008, 14 x 18 x 9 inches

During the late 1800s, the Jersey cow played a huge role in the westward movement across America. In many cases, the cow trekking along behind the Conestoga wagon was critical to the very survival of the family. The image of pioneers and milk cows are inseparable, and I have longed to sculpt this relationship for many years.

While creating the commission for Blue Bell Creamery in 2006, of a little country girl leading a Jersey cow, I saw many compositions in addition to their brilliant logo. And my model for the "little country girl" grew 6 inches in one year and became a young woman. The faraway look of a teenage girl is as timeless as the Jersey Cow itself. The little girl that once did her morning chores with such determination now had other things on her mind

High Country Spring, 2007, 10 x 12 inches

Mountain Bouquet, 2008, 8 x 10 inches

Sculpture and Painting Comparison

My career began in the 1970's as a wildlife painter. I initially started sculpting as a means to learn animal anatomy. The challenges of working in three dimensions eventually won the conflict of finding time for both mediums. I began painting again intermittently while living in New Mexico. The beauty of Southwestern Colorado, is so inspiring, however, that I am once again working toward splitting my time between painting and sculpture.

Many of the same principles apply to both mediums. It did take a while, but I can now go between the two mediums comfortably. The change from sculpture to painting and back to sculpture keeps me fresh and excited. Composition, dynamic lines, negative spaces, and light and shadow are all considerations for both painters and sculptors.

Sculpture has the added challenge of needing to incorporate these elements from 360 degrees as well as from the top and the bottom. This makes the process much more time-consuming. A limb, a head, and a torso are "drawn" from every conceivable angle. A change on one side affects the other sides. Symmetry is vital. It takes months to get it just right, and during the process the sculptor must strive for accuracy without losing sight of the original inspiration. They must maintain a balance between scientific and emotional honesty during the long process.

Painting is a refreshing change, particularly plein air painting. The canvas panels are small because you only have two to three hours to capture the scene before the light has changed too dramatically. This limited time is very intense. There is no group of people quieter than several artists standing near each other painting a landscape.

When a subject inspires me to paint, it is because I am seeing light. The subject is usually at least thirty feet away. Painting is an illusion. The challenge comes in taking paint and creating a sense of light and an illusion of three dimensions on a two dimensional surface. It is a challenging balance to get the correct value when striving for the correct color and color temperature.

When a subject inspires a sculpture, it is usually because I am physically closer to the subject. Movement as seen from the distance is certainly an important part of the inspiration, but being close enough to touch my subject is what gets me truly excited. This is where I observe the form and see the planes that make that form unique.

Radar, 2008, 12 1/2 x 13 x 5 inches

The humble little burro has been a favorite subject for both painting and sculpture throughout my career. I am fortunate to have several great models nearby. "Radar" was sculpted outdoors under the critical supervision of another burro, Angus, and their pal, Hank the Percheron.

Radar and Angus, 12 x 12 inches
Exhibited at the 2009 *Masters of the American West*
Autry National Center, Los Angeles, California

Sculpture is factual. The third dimension is created directly. I still, however, rely on illusion to convey a sense of lightness to surfaces such as hair, feathers and fabric.

Varying textures are important to both sculptors and painters. For example, smoothly sculpted or painted surfaces can be used to indicate where a bone comes close to the surface such as a cheekbone or the point of a shoulder. Texture also plays a role in creating "values."

"Values" from white to black are imperative to the success of both mediums. When sculpting, values are created by building out the form to catch light or by cutting into the surface to create shadows. Painters use values, color and color temperature to create high or low forms. Recognizing that colors become lighter and cooler as they recede into the distance allows a painter to manipulate the paint to create sense of high and low forms.

"Massing" is imperative in both sculpture and painting. Hair, for instance, is most effective when it is not painted or sculpted strand for strand, but when it is massed. Planes, rather than strands of hair, are utilized to indicate the form. This principle applies to all of nature's fine textures such as grass and leaves.

"Lost edges" are used in both mediums to indicate softness. This is effective in sculpture where the brow line disappears against the face or where hair is wispy. Lost or softened edges in a painting help make a flat surface appear round or a cloud to appear fluffy.

When I was young, still in my teens, I recognized the need to understand animal anatomy. Like many of my contemporaries faced with the abstract art movement of the 1960's, I had to learn many of the fundamentals on my own. I turned to sculpture to educate myself about anatomy so I could be a better painter.

I believe with my whole heart that an understanding of anatomy and the third dimension is the key to the treasure chest of creativity. Today both mediums are part of my daily creative life, and I dip into that treasure chest of knowledge every single time I touch clay or a paintbrush.

Mouse on the Menu, 2009, 10 x 13 1/2 x 5 1/2 inches

Jenny, 2009

Disappearing, 2010, 10 x 18 inches

I found a recently killed red fox along the road enroute to having my hair done. I gathered the already decaying carcass in a towel and put it in the back of my Tahoe. The unfortunate fox was then taken to a nearby friend's home so I could get measurements. It was then buried so it could be retrieved later and added to my collection of bones. Coincidentally, my friends David and Pati Temple, had been feeding a young fox that past winter. She introduced me to "Jenny" and Jenny ended up inspiring *Mouse on the Menu* as well as several paintings and drawings.

The Visitor, 2009, 9 x 12 inches

Lilies and Aspen, 2007, 12 x 12 inches

Collaboration

Bronze sculpture is not a singular endeavor. An artist must rely on the talents of many craftsmen if they are to see their clay model in its final and permanent form of bronze.

As mentioned earlier, I began sculpting to gain a better understanding of anatomy to improve my paintings. Sculpture definitely served this purpose, but it became much more than a means to an end. Sculpture for the sake of sculpture became my sole medium for two decades.

In 1972, a metallurgic engineer, Bob Zimmerman, converted an industrial foundry in Loveland, Colorado, to a bronze fine art foundry. Bob and his wife Mary thereby opened a door for artists like myself to cast our clay models in bronze. They provided all the services needed from mold making through patina.

I cast my first bronze, a single bighorn ram, creatively titled *Bighorn Ram* in an edition of 10. It sold out immediately and this success naturally encouraged me to continue sculpting. I recall that for six years I was torn between painting and sculpture and eventually set the painting aside.

Since casting my first bronze in 1973, I have worked with many artisans and foundries. During the "oil boom" of the mid 1980's, sculpture was in such demand that Loveland Art Castings could not keep up with my production needs. Several of us who had attained success realized that we needed to have our own finishing foundries and employees to fulfill the demand for our work.

This demand also caused several artisans trained at Loveland Art Castings to open their own businesses. Loveland, Colorado became a sculpture community of mold makers, wax chasers, companies specializing in wood and stone bases and even individuals who specialize in patinas. The more demanding art of casting bronze still required the knowledge of someone like Bob Zimmerman.

I purchased an industrial building in Englewood, Colorado, a few miles from my home and installed a new sand blaster and air compressor. I built a refrigerated room for waxes and a wax pouring and chasing area. The metal chasing room was sound proofed and had good air circulation. There was a nice office at the front. I hired an office manager, a metal chaser, and a wax person. A large and brightly lit room served as a studio where I sculpted my first monument, *Old Maude*.

This ideal set up, however, was short-lived. Joe and I separated just after I finished sculpting *Old Maude*. I was lost for a short while, searching for a new home and a new life. I wanted to live in the mountains, and Jackson Hole, Wyoming was my first goal. The severe winters, however, precluded an equally important goal of having more time for horses. There also was not a foundry within a reasonable distance. Then I discovered a charming log home overlooking the Plum Creek Valley south of Denver, just west of Castle Rock. I purchased the house, converted the barn into a studio and installed my foundry equipment and office in the lower level of the house.

Hiring Dimitry Spiridon in 1985, to do metal chasing, welding, and patinas, proved to be one of the best decisions of my career. When I moved to Santa Fe, Dimitry followed. I gave him my foundry equipment, and he started his own bronze-finishing business, Domani Bronze. In March 2010, Dimitry and his wife Nadine, followed Roger and me back to Colorado. Dimitry is now able to offer artists in the Four Corners region the same opportunities to create bronze that launched my own career in Loveland in the 1970's.

Dimitry and I work well together through the inherent problems of bronze. So many things can and do go wrong during the process. It is helpful, if not imperative, for the sculptor go over the wax model before it is cast and to work with the metal chaser and "approve the metal" before the patina is applied. If an artist doesn't do their own patina, they need to work closely with the patineur and again "approve the patina" before the final protective coat of wax is applied. The one whose signature is on the bronze is ultimately responsible for the final work of art. "The foundry did it wrong" is not an acceptable excuse.

On March 17, 1978, Dimitry Spiridon and five of his friends swam the freezing Danube River from Romania to Yugoslavia. They only got five miles inside what was then the Yugoslavian border before being captured on March 18 at 2:30 in the morning. At 8:00 that morning a judge sentenced them to 1 1/2 years in prison for illegally entering the country. One year and two months later, they were taken to the Austrian border where they were given a police escort to a refugee camp. Dimitry's dream to come to America was realized in October 1981 when he was sent to California.

Dimitry had been interested in art in Romania, so he actively sought work in art foundries to learn the process. It was his good fortune to have Romanian friends in the United States who were already working in art foundries and could help him overcome the initial language barriers. His first job was in a California foundry. From there he moved to Salt Lake City and worked briefly at Ed Fraughton's foundry.

I met Dimitry in Denver where he was working for International Fine Arts Foundry. By this time he had become familiar with the entire casting process and was quite accomplished at welding and metal chasing.

Dimitry Spiridon with a partially completed casting of *A New Beginning*. The raw bronze is shiny from chasing and sanding. It is sandblasted prior to applying the chemical patina.

A New Beginning, working model, 2005, 14 x 14 x 9 inches

Creating a Life-Sized Bronze Sculpture

A NEW BEGINNING — CONCEPT TO COMPLETION

A New Beginning portrays a Victorian woman in the 1890's. She is self-assured and ready to take full advantage of the opportunities of the decade. In 1890, Wyoming entered the union as the first state to allow women the right to vote. Colorado followed their lead, and in 1893 became the first state to legislate women's vote.

Seamstress Ricci Dawson of Mrs. Camp's Town Ladies, a Durango-based group who celebrate Victorian history, provided authenticity with her 1890's traveling suit, parasol and carpetbag. My studio assistant and director of Goodnight Trail Gallery, Jamie Bade, modeled for the sculpture.

A New Beginning represents the empowerment women felt in the 1890's.

Carol Lee Veitch, Kathy L'Amour and Susan Brown came to see the final clay of *A New Beginning* before it was cast. Here it has been pushed out into the sunlight for final adjustments.

THE MONUMENT STUDIO

Creating large sculptures takes space. The north end of our barn was designed for the unique needs of sculpture. The room is 24 by 36 feet with a 17 foot high ceiling. The smooth cement floor makes it easy to roll sculpture stands and pallets around and the clay scrapes off easily. There is a balcony that allows me to look down on large works to confirm symmetry. There are two large north windows and good overhead lights. A "model run" to the west allows me to work from life. The best part of this studio, however, is the overhead garage door that connects the studio to the barn aisle. I can push the sculpture outdoors into full sunlight and observe it from a distance. While details are a very important element of my work, the silhouette of the sculpture has to read correctly from a distance and the shadows have to make the large simple forms easily understood.

PATINA

The final stage is the application of chemicals to achieve the given colors I have chosen. This color is referred to as the "Patina." The bronze is heated to several hundred degrees and the chemicals are applied. The heat "opens" the metal to accept the chemicals. This process permanently changes the color of the surface of the bronze.

Several coats of wax are then applied to the surface. Each coat is buffed before applying the next coat of wax. The application of wax not only gives added depth to the patina, it protects the sculpture from weather.

The Cheyenne Frontier Days Old West Museum raised funds to keep the Number One casting of *A New Beginning* in Cheyenne, "to celebrate the history of Wyoming and the role of Wyoming women in creating the society we enjoy today." This is an incredibly appropriate placement, for in 1869, the Territory of Wyoming was the first to provide women the right to vote. In 1890, Wyoming became the first state to grant women the right to vote.

THE FINISHED SCULPTURE
A New Beginning,
life-size, 2009,
76 x 30 x 37 inches

Ready to Ride

Photographs and artistic depictions in the early 1900's often showed very attractive women in large Stetson hats and elaborate gauntlet gloves. There was a sense of romance in the clear western air, and the women thrived on freedom from Victorian attitudes.

Women's rights, going from side saddles to riding astride, and the evolution to practical clothing went hand in hand during the late 1800's and early 1900's. Change, of course, doesn't happen overnight and is often measured in small increments. Confining corsets, long flowing dresses and sidesaddles kept women dependent. The split riding skirt was a major stepping-stone toward independence. It allowed a woman to ride in a much more comfortable and safe position astride the horse. When she dismounted, however, the front of the skirt could be buttoned closed in to avoid offending those who were not yet enlightened.

Ready To Ride, 2010, 24 x 9 x 9 inches

Dust Devil, 2010, 23 x 18 x 11 inches

*San Juan Summer,*2010, 10 x 12 inches

Summer Storm, 2010, 10 x 12 inches

Rivers Edge, 2009, 10 x 12 inches

At Rest, 2010, 10 x 12 inches
Exhibited at the 2011 *Masters of the American West*
Autry National Center, Los Angeles, California

Visiting the Ancients, Long House Ruin — Mesa Verde National Park, 2010, 14 x 18 inches

May 2010 I was issued a Special Use Permit for myself and eight other artists to paint along Wetherill Mesa in Mesa Verde National Park. We were allowed free access to the Mesa without the distraction of tourists. The second day was unprecedented in that we were allowed to paint from inside Long House Ruin. It was an extraordinary experience made even better because it was shared with great artists who have been friends for many years.

Rising Steam, 2010, 12 x 16 inches

"Always in any group of animals, whether
men or beasts, certain individuals emerge."
J. Frank Dobie 1941

204

Old Blue

Eleven million head of cattle were driven north from Texas between 1865 and 1874. This was the largest migration of animals under the direction of man in the history of the world and many of the drovers became American legends.

My ancestor, Colonel Charles Goodnight, is one of those legends. His biographer, Evetts Haley, writes that Goodnight didn't give a hoot for his own legacy but he wanted everyone to know of the feats of his remarkable lead steer, Old Blue.

Goodnight's friend, J. Frank Dobie, took up the cause and tells Blue's story in his classic book "The Longhorns," written in 1941. Dobie writes "Old Blue was known from the Pecos to the Arkansas, in Colorado as well as in Texas. He knew the trail to Dodge City better than hundreds of cowboys who galloped up Front Street."

Old Blue died in 1890 at the age of 20. For many years his horns hung over the office door of the JA Headquarters at the Palo Duro Canyon. Today they can be seen in The Panhandle Plains Museum in Canyon, Texas. These horns weren't huge by twenty-first century standards, but the were a classic shape and it was Old Blue's legend that grew to great lengths.

Old Blue was so tame that he was fitted with a leather neck strap and a shiny brass bell. The steers soon learned to follow the sound of Blue's bell. A little strap was attached to quiet the bell clabber at night. Dobie states that when it was time to travel, Blue would nose his way to one of the point men to have the clapper loosened. "He would give a toss of head, and a switch of his tail, and head north."

It is this attitude, the attitude of a leader who loves his job, which I set out to capture in bronze.

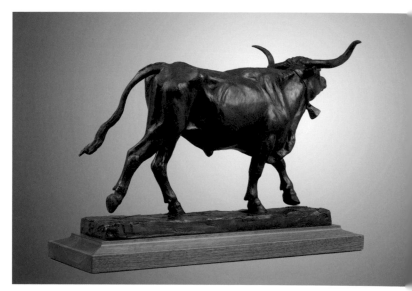

Blue's brass bell and strap are permanently displayed at the Cattle Raisers Museum in Forth Worth, Texas. Well known Western singer and cowboy poet, Red Steagall, has written a poem called *The Bell of Old Blue*.

Colonel Goodnight's wish has been fulfilled. More than a century after Old Blue's death, his legend remains alive in museums, in song, and in bronze.

Old Blue, 2010, 14 x 21 x 11 inches

The Journey Continues

The little town of Mancos, Colorado, has proved itself to be "on the way" rather than "out of the way." Mancos is situated on the San Juan Scenic Byway between the resort community of Durango, Colorado, 25 miles to the east, and the entrance to Mesa Verde National Park, just six miles to the west.

The Mancos Valley has a rich cultural history dating back to the Ancestral Puebloans. There are literally thousands of ancient Indian ruins within a few hour's drive to stir one's imagination. Many of the rivers and mountains were named by Spanish explorers. The Ute and Navajo tribes have a strong presence in the region to this day. The Wetherill family, Quaker cattle ranchers famous for bringing the fabulous Indian ruins of Mesa Verde to the attention of the public, settled south of the present town of Mancos in 1879. And, very much to my surprise, one of the original settlers in 1875 was John Wesley Sheek, Charles Goodnight's stepbrother, who was his first partner during Goodnight's cattle driving years.

Mancos has a perfect blend of the new and the old. The valley attracts its share of nature lovers and outdoor sports enthusiasts. But at its core are generations of working folks - folks with dirt under their nails - ranchers, cowboys and lumberjacks. It is an open-minded and supportive community, with diversity that fires the imagination. This is real Louis L'Amour Country – a land woven with rich history from its mountain peaks to its red rock canyons.

My own dogs, horses, and other charges have always inspired my work. They have taught me that every animal is as individual as you and me. They make me laugh and cry and question my own relationship to every living thing. After years of studying the anatomy of a horse, a dog, a buffalo – I learned that they have the same bones, the same muscles, and the same internal organs as humans. Through hours spent with many animals, I have seen them love, hate, and grieve just as we do. I watch them communicate in ways humans cannot comprehend. And I know that if I have a soul, so do they. Hopefully, through my art, I have been able to express these feelings and observations.

It is this belief,
combined with the beauty of the Rocky Mountains
and the uniquely American story
of settling the West,
that will fuel my journey
for as long as possible.

Acknowledgements

In addition to those named in the book, I wish to give special recognition to many who have supported and encouraged me over the years.

FAMILY
Roger Brooks
Dale and Rose Goodnight
Adam Goodnight
Grace Goodnight
Dean Goodnight
Bruce and Sally Goodnight
Sean and Leslie Branney
Scott and Judy Branney

FRIENDS
I have been blessed with far too many friends to list, but you know who you are. I thank you from the bottom of my heart for always being there.

MODELS
Some models brought a special energy to my work and I used them in many pieces.
Jessica La Casse
No Turning Back, The Gathering, Back From the Brink, As the Seasons Change, Mending the Flag
Kari Taylor
Looks Are Deceiving and *Passing Times*
Kathleen Owegone
Passing Times, Bathing Along the Pecos, The Birthday Pony
Jamie Bade
A New Beginning, Ready to Ride
Robin
Shepherds of the High Plains, Shepherds of the Nation, Team Ropers, Working Girl
Gwalowa
Into the Wind, What Friends Are For, Childhood Friends
Matt Dillion
Reflections, Running the Chapperal, Second Thoughts, High Expectations, American Warrior

ARTISTS
Artists are vital to each others careers. Many who have helped and influenced my work are gone. Others are now younger and inspiring me with their own fresh visions and enthusiasm. I have many friends among my contemporaries who I hold in very high regard. I mention only one, Patsy Davis. Because she constantly challenges herself, and inspires me with her own extraordinary talent and passion for sculpture.

ORGANIZATIONS
Society of Animal Artists
www.societyofanimalartists.com

The National Sculpture Society
www.nationalsculpture.org

Western Rendezvous of Art (NWR)
www.westrendart.org

GALLERIES
Trailside Gallery
Jackson, Wyoming and Scottsdale, Arizona
www.trailsidegalleries.com
Ginger Renner, Ted and Christine Mollring
Maryvonne Leshe, Joan Griffin and Kim Fletcher

Medicine Man Gallery
Santa Fe, New Mexico and Tucson, Arizona
www.medicinemangallery.com
Mark and Kathleen Sublette

Whistle Pik Gallery
Fredericksburg, Texas
www.whistlepik.com
Tim and Pamela Taylor

Goodnight Trail Gallery of Western Art
Mancos, Colorado
www.goodnighttrailgallery.com
Roger Brooks and Jamie Bade

Saks Gallery
Denver, Colorado
www.saksgalleries.com
Mikkel and Catherine Saks

Hayden Hays Gallery
Colorado Springs, Colorado
www.haydenhaysgallery.com
John Marzolf

Past Representation for which I remain grateful
Altermann and Morris Gallery
Formerly in Texas
Tony Altermann and Jack Morris

MUSEUMS HOSTING ANNUAL EXHIBITS
The Autry National Center
Masters of the American West
Los Angeles, California
theautry.org

Booth Western Art Museum
Catersville, Georgia
www.boothmuseum.org
Seth Hopkins, Executive Director

Desert Caballeros Museum
Cowgirl Up
Wickenburg, Arizona
www.westernmuseum.org

Eiteljorg Museum
Quest for The West
Indianapolis, Indiana
www.eiteljorg.org

The Cowgirl Hall of Fame
Heart of the West
Fort Worth, Texas
www.cowgirl.net

Haley Memorial Library and History Center
Midland, Texas
www.haleylibrary.com

Cheyenne Frontier Days Old West Museum
Cheyenne Frontier Days Governor's Invitational
Cheyenne, Wyoming
www.oldwestmuseum.org

Panhandle-Plains Historical Museum
Panhandle Plains Invitational Western Art Show and Sale
Canyon, Texas
www.panhandleplains.org

Thomas Gilcrease Museum
2011 Rendezvous Retrospective
Tulsa, Oklahoma
www.gilcrease.utulsa.edu

Colorado History Museum
Artists of America
Denver, Colorado
www.coloradohistory.org

Bennington Center for the Arts
Art and the Animal Kingdom
Bennington, Vermont
www.benningtoncenterforthearts.org

The National Museum of Wildlife Art
Western Visions
Jackson, Wyoming
www.wildlifeart.org

The Wildlife Experience Museum
Society of Animals Artist Annual Exhibit
Colorado Gold
Parker, Colorado
www.thewildlifeexperience.org

COLLECTORS
Without the financial support of collectors, an artist cannot afford to produce new work. I thank each and everyone who has purchased even the smallest of my work.

PATRONS
A patron goes beyond occasional collecting. They purchase a large amount of an artists work and often place that work in public places. Other patrons are instrumental in having an artists work recognized Nationally or Internationally. Collectors become patrons by using their personal collections as the foundation for a Museum.

Frances Crane Becker	David and Gail Lininger
Steve and Doris Colgate	Mac and Babs McKnight
Bill and Sandra Condon	John and Joan Mitchell
Dick Freed	Takeharu Miyama
Davis and Gwen Ford	Joe and Betty Moore
John and Saralynn Geraghty	John Painter
John and Jeanne Greene	Wayne and Andrea Rumley

Erivan and Helga Haub
Doris Heckerman
Jerry and Kay Jessen
Mike Kammerer
Bill and Joffa Kerr
John Koontz
Kathy L'Amour

Wayne and Andrea Rumley
Stan and Lorna Searle
Preston and Carolyn Smith
Dick and Audrey Stermer
Ed and Lynne Trumble
Hans von Barby
Grant and Marlena Wilkins

FOUNDRY SUPPORT
Art Castings of Colorado
Loveland, Colorado

Eagle Bronze
Lander, Wyoming

Land's End Sculpture Center
Paonia, Colorado
Bob and Mary Zimmerman

Madd Castings
Berthoud, Colorado

Shidoni Foundry
Santa Fe, New Mexico

Mark Toma Mold Making
Santa Fe, New Mexico

Brett Chomer Mold Making and Enlargement
Santa Fe, New Mexico

Domani Bronze
Cortez, Colorado
Dimitry Spiridon

Valley Bronze
Joseph, Oregon

PUBLICATIONS
I am grateful for the many articles that have been written by creative writers for newspapers and special interest publications. Special recognition goes to the magazines devoted to Art.

Art of the West
Allan and Elaine Duerr
Tom and Lori Tierney
For covering my work nine times to date
And for their relentless dedication to Western Art

Southwest Art
For numerous articles and including my work in a book titled *Sculptors of the Rockies*

Western Art Collector
For an eight page article written by John Geraghty that featured creating *A New Beginning*

Art Talk
Shari Morrison

Western Horseman
Kathy Swan

BOOKS
A Brush With the West -1980
Dale Burk

A Comprehensive Guide to Sculpture in Texas – 1996
Carol Morris Little

Leading the West – 1997
Donald J. Hagerty

An Encyclopedia of Women Artists of the American West – 1998
Phil Kovinick

The Revolution in Horsemanship - 2005
Robert M. Miller, D. V M. and Rick Lamb

A Buffalo In the House - 2007
Richard Rosen

Sculpture of the Rockies - 2010
Southwest Art Magazine

PHOTOGRAPHERS
Paul Boyer, Director of Photography

Marsha BonDurant
Roger Brooks
Jim Digby
Haley Memorial Library Archives
Edward Hopper III
Bob Lindholm
Anna Malarich, Brookgreen Gardens
Chris Marona

Wendy Shatill
Steve Sykes
Claude Steelman
Lou Swenson
Barbara van Cleve
Mike White
Sandi Whitmore
Carolyn Wright

213

Selected Public Collections and Monuments

A New Beginning
2011   Cheyenne, Wyoming

Back from The Brink (ten percent over life-size)
2003   The Wildlife Experience Museum – Denver, Colorado
2007   Museum of the Southwest – Midland, Texas
2007   Camp Tecumseh YMCA – Brookston, Indiana
2007   St. Frances Medical Center – Grand Island, Nebraska

Blue Bell Cow and Girl (life-size)
2007   Blue Bell Creamery, Brenham, Texas

Cares For Her Brothers (life-size)
1986   Brookgreen Gardens – Murrells Inlet, South Carolina
1988   Denver Zoo – Denver, Colorado

Mare Jumping Up (One and one quarter life-size)
1994   Western Michigan University – Kalamazoo, Michigan
1995   University of Texas – Austin, Texas

No Turning Back (life-size)
1997   Hirshfeld-Moore House – Texas A&M University
       Austin, Texas
1997   Old West Museum – Cheyenne, Wyoming
1999   City Hall – St. Joseph, Missouri
2002   University of Nebraska – Lincoln, Nebraska

Old Maude (life-size)
1982   Haley Memorial Library and History Center –
       Midland, Texas

Paint Mare and Filly (life-size)
1988   National Cowboy & Western Heritage Museum –
       Oklahoma City, Oklahoma

Passing Times
1994   International Museum of the Horse – Lexington, Kentucky
1994   Hubbard Museum of the American West –
       Ruidoso, New Mexico

1999   Metro National Plaza – Houston, Texas
1997   Hirshfeld-Moore House, Texas A&M University –
          Austin, Texas
2000   National Cowgirl Museum and Hall of Fame –
          Ft. Worth, Texas
2006   Booth Western Art Museum – Carterville, Georgia

Second Thoughts (life -size)
    2007   St. Frances Medical Center – Grand Island, Nebraska

Spring and Sprite (ten percent over life-size)
    2000   Old West Museum – Cheyenne, Wyoming
             City of Westcliffe – Westcliffe, Colorado
    2010   City of Woodside – Woodside, California

Stallion with Mare (One and one quarter life-size)
    1992   The Shelton – Dallas, Texas

Team Ropers (one and one half life-size)
    1991   Pro Rodeo Hall of Fame Museum – Colorado Springs,
             Colorado
    1991   Houston Astrodome – Houston, Texas
    1998   Stroh Ranch – Parker, Colorado

The Bronc (one and one quarter life-size)
    2002   University of Texas-Pan American – Edinburg, Texas
    2005   The Wildlife Experience Museum – Denver, Colorado

The Day The Wall Came Down (twenty-five percent over life-size)
    1997   George H. W. Bush Presidential Library –
             College Station, Texas
    1998   Allied Museum – Berlin, Germany

The Day The Wall Came Down (one quarter life-size working model)
    2004   Central Intelligence Agency – Washington, D. C. (maquette)
    2004   Ronald Reagan Presidential Library – Simi Valley, California
             (maquette)

The Freedom Horses (Five one and one quarter life-size)
    1992   Lely Resort – Naples, Florida

Wolf Pack (fifteen percent over life-size)
    2004   Lincoln Park Zoo – Chicago, Illinois
    2005   The Wildlife Experience Museum – Denver, Colorado
    2005   The Leanin' Tree Museum – Boulder, Colorado